Celtic Mythology

A Complete Guide to Celtic Mythology, Celtic Gods, and Celtic Folklore

Andrew Walsh

Table of Contents

Introduction 1

Chapter 1: The Importance of Celtic Culture 3

Chapter 2: The Diversity of Celtic Culture 16

Chapter 3: Celtic Religion 25

Chapter 4: Celtic Deities and Creatures 45

Chapter 5: Celtic Stories 91

Chapter 6: The Lingering Influence of Celtic Myths 115

Conclusion 122

Introduction

Congratulations on purchasing this book on *Celtic Mythology,* and thank you for doing so. If you're looking for a beginner's guide on Celtic culture, look no further. While this book focuses on mythology, it will also highlight other essential information about Celtic culture both in the past and present.

Throughout the following chapters, we will discuss Celtic people and the gods, goddesses, creatures, and lore that are most associated with Celtic culture. This book will also tell you about the diverse culture of Celts, where Celtic people originally came from, what makes a person Celtic, and about the Celtic religion beyond just the deities that were so important to the religion. You will learn why these myths continue to be important for modern Celts who no longer practice the Celtic religion but still hold onto many of the Celtic traditions.

In various countries such as Ireland, Scotland, and Wales, Celtic traditions are still vital in the identity of their citizens and shape their lives in ways that you might not have considered. Even in the United States, we see bits of Celtic culture influencing arts, music, and even sports.

Celtic Mythology will give you a new understanding of the word Celtic and clarify any misunderstandings you may have about the term. Most importantly, it will show you the joy of Celtic myths and mythical figures.

Thanks again for choosing this book. I hope you enjoy it!

Chapter 1: The Importance of Celtic Culture

Celtic Beauty

There's so much to love about the Celtic culture; it incorporates legends and myths of so many unique but interconnected places. Unfortunately, too few people even know that Celtic myths exist, or don't realize how integral they are in current cultures around the world. What comes to mind when you think Celtic? Most likely, you think of Ireland, or maybe Scotland. Perhaps, you think of Celtic art that is shaped so that it looks like an elaborate knot, or you think of the musical group Celtic Women, or maybe you think of a sports team like the Boston Celtics. Whatever it is that you think when you hear the word Celtic, it probably doesn't embody the full breadth of this diverse, beautiful culture.

Many people don't realize that Celtic people have their own mythology and a large collection of gods who they worshipped. When people think of polytheistic religions, their mind usually goes to the Greek, or Roman deities, which is understandable because of how immensely influential these two cultures were. However, Celtic myths are some of the most fascinating and vibrant tales of all, and you may even have heard of some of them before without realizing that they were Celtic.

Art, music, holidays, and other elements of Celtic culture are still appreciated by many and continue to bring joy and connection to people. Literature in Britain, France, Scotland, and Ireland, among other places, has been influenced by Celtic myths and traditions. While the Celtic myths weren't written down during their time, they were passed on, and they were incorporated in Christian works for centuries after the Celtic religion had been taken over because of the Roman conquest. The pagan Celtic religion is dead now, but it is not forgotten. Its practices are continued, and they live on through timeless legends.

The Celtic culture is rich and full of vibrant tales that are sure to appeal to anyone with an imaginative soul. It has inspired and influenced art, literature, and much more.

Who Are the Celtic People?

It's hard to say when precisely the Celtic people became Celts, but there are estimates of when early Celtic people began to appear. It is believed that Celtic people functioned in tribes beginning around 1200 BCE, but it took some time before they were called Celtic. The name Celtic was first uttered by Julius Caesar, who came across Celtic people and called them Celtae. English speakers did not use the word Celtic to describe the Celtic people until the eighteenth century, at which time linguists were able to find the link between Celtic people:

language. Thus, when the languages were connected, the term Celtic was finally established to describe the group of tribes who spoke that shared group of languages.

Today, Celtic culture is associated with countries like Scotland, Wales, Ireland, and the Isle of Man as well as other Celtic nations that still rely heavily on Celtic languages and cultural elements, even with other predominant cultures surrounding them. Though, the exact nature of what defines Celtic people is still being discussed by researchers. Generally, the main areas for Celtic culture are in the United Kingdom as well as Northern France, where the culture is still important. Celtic tribes would eventually emigrate to places like Turkey and Portugal. Celtic culture would even have some influence on the Romans, but the Romans, of course, had their own religion, so the influence of the Celts on the Romans was limited. Nevertheless, the influence of the Celtic people and their traditions should not be understated because they had and still have a profound role in the world.

Two predominant theories postulate the ancestry of Celtic people. These theories speak to the archeological discussion of who is Celtic rather than the theistic one, so while there are no sure bets in this area, the digging up of Celtic remains has made some suggestions about where Celts originally came from and how their bodies tended to be. Much of this research shows how diverse the Celtic population was and how, based on the area of a specific tribe, the people would look very different from one another despite many similarities in culture.

The first theory suggests the Celts are of the Alpin race that was found in central Europe during the Neolithic period. These people moved from Africa or Asia and are found in some regions of modern France, Germany, and Scandinavia in Slavic populations. Through their travel, they spread their culture and language, leading to the development of Celtic language and traditions. They spread their culture and ancestry to Ireland, Britain, and Wales, among other Celtic places.

A second theory assumes that the Celtic religion originated in areas like Ireland and Asia minor, beginning in Teutonic tribes before spreading to more cultures. It's hard to say whether there is enough information to substantiate this theory, but given reports of the Celts being fair-haired, and the way that Romans have described them, this theory is a possibility. Regardless, it does seem that at one time, Celts may have had specific ancestry. Over time, they became more of a mixed-race, accounting for the differing types of skulls that archeologists have found among Celtic regions, as well as the differing complexions and builds of the people.

No matter what their early heritage, Celts can include any people who shared similar religions and cultural practices during BCE times and early CE. times before the spread of

Christianity would destroy much of the Celtic traditions and oral storytelling. While we don't know where the Celtic people initially came from, we have a better idea of where they were when Celtic traditions started to develop.

Celtic culture is estimated to have begun in the Late Bronze Age, showing up first in the Danube area. Before they started speaking Celtic languages, people used proto-Celtic language that would evolve into the poetic Celtic tongues that are associated with Celtic culture. Early Celtic people were called Urnfield people. As a result of iron replacing bronze in 800 BCE, a culture called the Hallstatt culture emerged, and ushered in a transition to the La Tene culture in 500 BCE. This culture thrived in central Europe, allowing them to take on the predominant Mediterranean forces. It was during this time of prosperity that these people were first called Celtic.

The Celtic religion began to spread as the Celtic tribes tried to escape both the wrath of Julius Caesar around the year 100 BCE, and that of Germanic tribes who sought to take over Celtic lands. They were driven from places such as Gaul, which is modern-day France, to new areas such as Asia, which is why Celtic roots can be found in so many different places in the world in select areas. The Brittany region of France, for example, still carries many Celtic traditions and speaks a Celtic language known as Breton, which is not seen in the rest of France.

The tribes became more engrained in world affairs as they became major warriors. They were often hired by other nations to fight battles. They were known for being good with horses and chariots and their abilities with javelins. Even Julius Caesar admitted how adept the Celtic warriors were. The Celtic soldiers were known for keeping their hair long, and having strong, stocky bodies. Based on Greek artwork, they used long, wooden shields that were unique from other shields that were being used during that period. Unfortunately, the Celtic armies were often outmatched, but they consistently put up a good fight and resisted being conquered.

The Celts settled in a myriad of regions, making their influence widespread in parts of Europe for several decades. Thus, even today, those with Celtic ancestry often take pride in their heritage and continue Celtic traditions, even if they do not subscribe to Celtic religions. Fortunately, the culture of the Celts is cherished by many who feel proud of their ancestors who practiced the Celtic religion and traditions. The languages of the Celts have not died, and while some dialects have evolved and some have become obsolete, Celtic words live on, which seems fitting given that most of the Celtic history we know today has been given to us via oral tradition rather than being written down.

It's also important to note that those in Celtic regions and who have Celtic ancestry can still be considered Celtic, so their myths and legends, which are slightly different from the early Celts, have become intertwined and culturally connective. Therefore, myths have evolved and taken on new lives with each generation that they have been passed down, which is true of any myths. Thus, Celts are both those people of the past and those people of the present. While this book primarily focuses on the myths originated by those who practiced the Celtic religion, many of these myths received facelifts upon the Christian invasion. Yet, the spirit of these stories is just as bright as ever. These stories deserve to shine on for many more generations. Accordingly, I want to spread these stories as much as I can to show the delightful, sometimes tragic, nature of Celtic myths because they are incredibly special.

What Are Myths?

Myths are a type of folklore that help to shape society. They often have supernatural elements and include gods, goddesses, and other mythical creatures that are regularly incorporated in pop culture. These mythical beings are usually placed into myths, and they engage in obstacles, heroics, tragedy, and other dramatized facets of life. Humans often play a role in the stories of these higher beings.

These myths are used to describe how the world came to be and how people behave. Myths about how the sun got into the sky or how mountains became mountains are common. In many cultures, pagan religions included gods related to the sun, the moon, and the weather. These myths helped to validate the religious and behavioral norms of the societies that they existed in. There are various definitions of what a myth is based on who you ask, but in the broadest sense of the term, they are traditional stories that have been passed down through generations. Myths are commonly differentiated from other folklore in that they have sacred origins. In Celtic countries, these religions include the Celtic religion itself as well as their Christian successors. Some of these myths have been secularized as they've been passed down.

Greek and Roman myths are some of the most common, but the expanse of cultures that had myths is endless. During the spread of the Roman empire, there were extensive groups that had various mythologies. These cultures had some overlap, but they all have unique and colorful stories that ancestors still hold onto dearly.

Why Myths Are Important

Celtic myths are a vital part of many people's cultures, but they can also be helpful to learn for those who don't have Celtic ancestry due to the cultural and historical significance of mythology in our world. Myths are crucial to the upbringings and ethical views of people around the world. All cultures have myths, and many of these myths have similar themes that drive them. These myths often preach morality and teach people right from wrong.

Some people wave off myths as just being fairytales that have no purpose in today's world. Others don't like myths because of religious connotations. Of course, many early myths were indeed related to religion, and many religions still utilize myths. Nevertheless, myths don't have to be religious at all. They used to be primarily religious, mostly because religion was one of the primary ways that people looked at society, which resulted in so many myths being tied in with religion.

Unfortunately, some people don't know enough about myths to see the benefits of them. They insist that they are people of reason and, therefore, that they don't need to hear tales of superstition. In the twentieth century, scholars started turning away from myths because they assumed that there was no need for them with increasing revelations in science. One scholar even called myths a language's disease. There have even been researchers like James Frazer, who tried to debunk myths. Frazer was a Scotsman, who determined in his book *The Golden Bough* that humans would move in a three-stage process that would go from thinking in terms of magic, to religion, to science. He decided that once people reached the scientific stage that primitive magic, and myths, would be useless. It's no wonder that in many Celtic countries, Celtic influences started to diminish for a while before being revived as important parts of those countries' cultures.

Psychologist Carl Jung determined that myths were a way that people could connect and engage within society. Meanwhile, Mircea Eliade, a Romanian theorist, agreed that myths could help people understand a complex world that would otherwise be very scary and conflicting. Through myths, people are able to establish societies and have shared values. Myths have also influenced the telling of history. Joseph Campbell took these ideas even further and detailed four ways in which myths were vital to society. In summation, he said that myths awed people, oriented religious beliefs, created social order, and provided spiritual enlightenment.

While our modern myths may not look precisely like the myths the Celts had, mediums that use Superheroes are essentially myths. We don't look at these stories as truth in any way, but these tales still shape our society and demonstrate societal and moral values. Comic books are commonly considered by scholars to be modern mythology. Further, science fiction and fantasy books like *Harry Potter* and the *Percy Jackson* series are beloved books that have mythical elements and use many of the same tropes or character types as classical mythology. These are modernized versions of the myths, but they are myths just the same and have wormed their way into the hearts of the modern generations. The surge of superhero films made from comics only go to show that we love myths.

We still spread these stories by word of mouth too. We tell our friends about them and talk about them when we go out to dinner. We give our reviews, and some people even write fanfiction about the characters that they love, truly throwing themselves into the mythological culture. Moreover, we still have fairytales of our own, and again, we are remaking them. Remakes of movies like Cinderella have become popular, and that tale itself is a composite of many similar mythological tales. Each Cinderella story from each culture is unique, and they reflect the time in which they are told. The modern Cinderella story has a happy ending to reflect Western tales of rags to riches and the American dream, while other cultures have less happy versions of this story. The point is that like it or not; myths are a part of us. Those fairytales we hear as children take on new forms. They grow and adapt, and we even make new stories based on those ideas, but myths are not going anywhere.

Classic stories, those myths that are somehow universal due to the variations that are found in every culture, still appeal to us, and today, they connect us with much more than just the people in our immediate culture. Thus, to say that the myth has become meaningless or should become meaningless is to say that there should be no more stories of princesses, superheroes, talking snowmen, or intergalactic battles. Early people used the stars or statues to represent these stories, and we use books and screens to accomplish that same goal. It doesn't matter if you are religious or not. The myths we have today teach values and highlight the norms of our society, and when we see fit, we can choose to resist these norms and create a new mythology, and that's the joy of myths. With every change, myths can shift to match those changes.

Myths are what build nations. Even now, all nations have myths that join them as people and interweave their stories together. These myths overarch societal structures and shape the decisions that people in these nations make. Humans are storytelling creatures. Can you go a day without telling a story, including little ones like telling your spouse about something that happened at work? For most people, the answer is probably not.

Myths teach people how to be imaginative as well. They establish mythical worlds that have elements that can't be seen and can only be imagined. This imagination is important because it allows you to think outside of the box and imagine greater things. It allows you to see beyond the surface level and think analytically.

Stories have long been associated with wisdom. In the Celtic culture, the druids were fundamentally the storytellers of their society, and these storytellers were also the intellectual elite because of how influential these stories were. To know the world, it helps to be able to look at it in fictional terms because when you can do so, you can look upon the world with empathy. Facts are helpful, and they are informative, but stories speak to the feelings that people have, which are crucial to how people behave. It doesn't matter how much people know because feelings like passion and anger can still sway them, and myths teach how to deal with those non-concrete feelings, and they allow humanity to remain humane.

Myths are still important to us today because they are still part of us. We are still intertwined in old myths. They shaped our ancestors, who in turn shaped us. Without myths, there would be less to connect people. Myths even connect people of other cultures because through stories, it is easier to understand each other and talk about each other's troubles.

The study of old myths is so rewarding because it shows humans where we came from. It highlights how we used to be and how we are now. Many of the old myths carry similar themes to new ones, meaning that learning the old myths helps us connect to our ancestors and helps our imaginations soar. Celtic myths are some of the most underrated historic myths out there, but they are so enriching. While times have changed, there's a universality to the Celtic myths that will entertain you even though some of the values have been replaced or shifted in today's Celtic culture.

Chapter 2: The Diversity of Celtic Culture

Celtic Cultures

Celtic people are not thought to be of one ethnicity or origin and were instead comprised of many tribes that, for some unclear reason, began to speak languages that were of the same family and had a lot of similarities. Even today, several hotspots show how diverse the Celtic culture was and still is. These six main areas where the Celtic language is still spoken show how Celts have adapted and shifted their ways while still embracing their Celtic roots.

One of the places that you can find Celtic culture even today is Brittany. Brittany is a province in northwestern France that has a unique culture compared to the rest of France. In Brittany, they combine French traditions with Celtic ones, and they still speak the Breton language locally. In France, they have a popular cartoon called Asterix the Gaul who, with his friends, battles the Roman Empire who invaded the area where the Gaul tribe had settled. This comic gives a glimpse of the unique culture that is found in Brittany because of its Celtic roots. The people of Brittany, called Bretons, love their heritage, and many of them associate with being Breton before they associate with being French. Yet, in the French system, their culture often is undermined and placed under French culture. Nevertheless,

Breton schools still teach the language, and the Bretons strive to keep their culture alive even as they are sometimes pushed to adopt more normalized French culture. In Brittany, the sounds of bagpipes and harps may more closely resemble Scottish culture than that of France. Bretons have also brought the genre of Celtic rock into fruition, and it has become a part of the French music scene. The region continues to hold festivals to celebrate their culture. One of the most prominent festivals they hold is the InterCeltique Festival that happens each year in August, which focuses on music. Brittany is a vibrant place that excellently encapsulated Celtic culture and continues to appreciate Celtic mythology.

Another place that still has a lot of Celtic culture is Cornwall. Cornwall is known for wool, linen, and sheepskin, all of which were used for shoes and clothing by Celtic people. These goods have a long history of being great objects of trade for the Celts, and the love for these goods has only deepened as people in Cornwall strive to maintain and revitalize the Celtic culture. Two tribes were known to have originated in Cornwall, the Cornovii, and the Dumnonii. These tribes lived in Cornwall even after the Roman Empire had fallen, and accordingly, have long been an important part of Cornwall's development. Anglo-Saxon invaders did not appreciate the Cornish culture, so for a while, much of the Celtic culture began to die. It had nearly died out by the turn of the eighteenth century; however, efforts have been made to revive Celtic traditions to celebrate the origins of the country. Some traditions have survived, such as the act of Cornish hurling, which is a game that has two teams try to keep a silvery ball in their possession. They also still hold festivals such as the 'Obby 'Oss Festival, which is held in downtown Padstow, where they have parades and other celebratory activities. Unfortunately, the language is still only spoken by a select few, with an estimated four hundred people that are fluent, but the government has been enacting programs to help increase these numbers.

Ireland is one of the cultures that is most linked to Celtic traditions. Many Irish traditions, even ones that are not overtly Celtic, are often referred to as Celtic because Celtic and modern Irish cultures are so enmeshed. Celtic music, Celtic designs, and the Celtic language are all things that the Irish take pride in. They also still celebrate many of the folklores that the original Celtic people handed down through the generations. Despite Christianity, particularly Catholicism, becoming prominent in Ireland, the folklore continued to be used. Early Christians maintained the Celtic folklore, switching it just a bit to further Christianity while still maintaining some of the old beliefs to appeal to the converts. The Irish merging of Christian and Celtic ideas can be seen throughout the world in places where the Irish emigrated to. With a long history of hardship and many fights for their autonomy, the Irish have long used myths to keep their spirits high and continue to use those myths to this day!

Wales maintains many Celtic locations that visitors can go to if they want to experience the nation's Celtic roots. In Wales, the original Celts disappeared in 43 AD when the Romans invaded, but their spirit and legends live on. Hillforts in Wales have been maintained to show how the Celts lived, and several Welsh museums have mementos from the Celts such as jewelry, hair accessories, combs, and razors. People in Wales also continue to learn and speak Welsh, which is one of the closest modern languages to the old-style Celtic languages. Festivals and celebrations can be found that emphasize the Celtic culture of Wales and show it to the next generation. There's no debate that the Celtic spirit is very much still alive in Wales as a source of pride and ancestral connection.

Isle of Man, like the other countries listed, is deeply influenced by Celtic culture, which has been merged with Anglican culture. For those of you who don't know, this British- dependent country is between Great Britain and Ireland, and it didn't have Gaelic influences until the year 500, at which time the Manx language emerged in the Isle of Man, which is the Gaelic language. While it's unclear where the name if this isle came from, many people associate the name with the Celtic god, Manannan Mac Lir, who was a sea god said to have protected the island by putting fog around it. Just from this fact alone, you can see how influential the Celtic legends are to the establishment of this island and the indoctrination of its people. While people do not commonly use the Gaelic language, it is still kept alive, and the language still influences how people on this island speak. Many of them sound more akin to Scottish or Irish people because of the continued influences of Gaelic in their speech. The Isle of Man is small, but it packs a big cultural punch!

Scotland is one of the most prominent Celtic nations. Scotland has even chosen the unicorn as its national animal, even though it is a mythical creature. This is because unicorns were important Celtic creatures that represent purity, power, and chivalry. The Celts in Scotland originate from two Celtic tribes, the Gaels and the Picts, who both founded Scotland in the ninth century. Thus, Celts have a foundational role in the creation of Scotland and all its political and social systems. Scotland has since been Christianized like the other lands that once followed the Celtic religion, but they still cherish their Celtic roots and strive to celebrate that part of their culture.

The cultures that remain filled with Celtic influences are all proud of their heritage because their Celtic roots are part of who they are. Imperial powers tried to dominate the Celtic culture and erase it to usher in Christianity. While only a select few countries maintain Celtic cultures, Celtic ideas are seen throughout the world in mythical creatures such as fairies. This Celtic culture is vital to the happiness and sense of fulfillment of many people, and the myths are thousands of years old, but they still entertain and teach people valuable life lessons.

Celtic Languages

The Celtic language was crucial to the storytelling culture that the Celts held. While the Celts did not write any of their myths or religious ideals down, they valued the act of memorizing stories and passing them through the generations. When Christians arrived, some select stories of the Celtic religions were passed down in writing, but even then, much of what was passed down was done so through oral storytelling. The only writing that the original Celts really did was using an alphabet called Ogham that they used to mark burial sites. With all that in mind, the oral tradition of Celtic language is one of the most important facets of the Celtic culture.

Interestingly, because the Celts didn't write their stories down, the Romans considered them to be snobs who didn't want their stories to become available to anyone who wanted to learn about them. Julius Caesar guessed that they didn't write their myths down because they wanted to keep druids in an elevated societal position. The Celts even knew Greek letters, showing that they were intelligent but dedicated to oral methods of learning, which makes the existing culture of Celts even more profound because it is so linked to people's ancestors and the process of handing down information as well as listening.

Celtic language is still spoken even now in countries or parts of countries with deep Celtic roots. While the Celts all share similar languages, their dialects and tribal languages varied greatly and evolved in different ways due to influences in the distinct parts of the world in which the tribes developed. The Celtic language is generally considered to be an Indo-European tongue, but some scholars suggest that the language may be closer linked to Hamito-Semitic languages because of the syntax of Celtic languages. If the latter is the case, it demonstrates how Celts were forced to use unfamiliar languages forced on them by dominant cultures, but they maintained their own syntax to make the unknown languages more sensible to them.

Celtic languages have also been divided into the categories of Continental Celtic and Insular Celtic. Continental Celtic refers to Celtic languages that people didn't speak once the Roman culture took over. We do not have much left of these languages because they only still exist in select works by Greeks or Romans that contain fragments of the language. Parts of these languages remain in epigraphs, pottery, and stelae.

Much of the Celtic languages have been obliterated by new languages that swept in and erased many of the Celtic roots, but in Brittany, Ireland, Scotland, Wales, Cornwall, and Isle of Man, some Celtic tongues are still spoken. These languages are the Insular Celtic languages, which were spoken even as the Roman Empire flourished. Two predominant branches of Celtic languages are preserved: Goidelic and Brythonic. Goidelic is known as Gaelic, while Brythonic is the British linguistic branch of Celtic languages. The Gaelic language is found in places like Ireland and the Scottish highlands. Meanwhile, the British branch is primarily found in Wales today, but while the Roman ruled, it was spoken in all of Britain. The Welsh language is one of the most prominent Celtic languages of all. The Welsh use this language as a way to separate their culture from the British and preserve their heritage that was stripped by colonialism.

Cornish stopped being spoken in the 1700s but has been reclaimed in more recent times. Breton was given by settlers who came to Britain in the fifth century, and Welsh is still a prominent language in Wales. As for the Gaelic languages, the most prominent example is the modern Irish language that has evolved into the language we know today.

In the United Kingdom, Celtic languages became somewhat stigmatized and were deemed lesser than the English language. Yet, plenty of Celtic words were taken by the English. Words like truant, slogan, flannel, car, and bucket all have Celtic roots. While often discouraged by Christian powers, Celtic languages are a source of pride for the people who hang onto them and bring them into modern times, and in select places, this language can be part of daily lives. Where it is not used standardly, the Celtic language doesn't tend to do well or be taught by schools.

Primarily, even in places that have scorned the public use of Celtic languages, geographical locations are still commonly connected to Celtic words in places where Celtic culture was once predominant. The Thames and London are both Celtic in origin. The towns of Lincoln and York are also Celtic in their roots. Interestingly, many places in Britain are named based on combined English and Celtic words. For example, Brewood in Staffordshire or Brill in Buckinghamshire both are made from English and Celtic words, showing the combining of the two cultures. Additionally, many British places use the word 'combe', which stems from a Celtic word that means valley, and the word 'tor' that is also used in British geography comes from the Celtic word for rock. These are only just a few of the ways that Celtic languages have infiltrated modern times, even in places that don't highly value Celtic traditions and speech.

While the Celtic languages are very much unused in many places that once used them, their influences have been intermixed with the cultures that overrun them. Celtic groups became part of the Anglo-Saxon culture; thus, as these two groups intermixed and even married each other, their traditions and certain expressions became intermingled. In many ways, parts of the Celtic language will always live on through other languages that embrace those Celtic elements, even if unwittingly. The Celtic languages are diverse, but they all fall under one category of languages that connect people and spread the Celtic traditions, particularly the folklores.

Chapter 3: Celtic Religion

Religion Overview

While many of the practices of Celtic religions are unknown because this information is lost, several conclusions have been made or suggested based on archeological and historical information. Remember that Celtic religions are diverse and were practiced uniquely in each region. The main connections between these areas were language and polytheistic religions that were unified by similar or shared gods. There are no accounts left by anyone who practiced Celtic religion, so we can't be certain exactly how each Celtic religion operated. We must try to piece together artifacts and second-hand information as best as possible to gain an understanding of how Celtic religion was practiced in various places. When you start to put the pieces together, you get a fascinating view of what early Celtic people did to celebrate their religious beliefs.

The Celts followed a calendar that split the year into Winter and Summer halves called the Calendar of Coligny. They had two important feast days that represented the middle of each season. The seasons can be seen in various myths and would be broken down into twelve months with an extra month every five years to account for the extra days left by the shortened months. Some days would be considered lucky, while others were called unlucky, showing the superstition of Celts. In the different seasons, they followed different rituals and appealed to different gods based on what they needed during an individual season.

From what we know, Celtic beliefs are similar, but not equivalent to, many better known polytheistic cultures like the Greeks and Romans. Even among the Celts, some of the practices vary; there's some degree of guesswork that we have to do because of the lack of information written down. Many of the Celtic Gods and Goddesses have similar roles to specific Greek or Roman gods or goddesses because while diverse, polytheistic religions often influenced one another and were based on the same basic tenets. Folktales were used to tell people how they should behave, teach them lessons, and introduce them to gods who were in charge of numerous important spheres in ancient and medieval life.

Druids played an important role in the Celtic religion and society at large. Druids were the priests of the Celtic religion and were of a high-ranking class in society. They had both religious and legal authority that made them important figures in Celtic countries. The most important part of their job was to learn the myths and pass the stories on, but they did also handle any disputes that required a judge. With so many hats, druids were busy, but they were admired and powerful. They were lucky in that they didn't have roles as warriors, nor did they have to pay taxes so they could stick to their duties as leaders within communities. Much of what we know about druids has been ascertained by archeologists as well as through the writings of Julius Caesar. The Celts kept no records of what the druids did. The word druid itself is etymologically linked to the Celtic word for a sacred oak tree because the oak tree was associated with wisdom. The druids not only studied religion and were superstitious, but they also studied philosophy. They also were always present during ritual sacrifices. Below the druids was a class called diviners, and beneath the class of diviners were ordinary bards.

In the fifth century A.D., Romans and Anglo-Saxons were both unable to conquer Ireland, so much of the religious culture thrived there compared to other locations that had less time to develop religious practices. However, in 432 AD, St. Patrick came into Ireland and the converting of the Irish to Catholicism began. As a result, many druids were hunted down and killed to get rid of the teachers of Celtic religion. Nevertheless, in Irish religion, some Celtic symbols were kept as Catholic, such as the Celtic cross and the shamrock.

In Celtic society, children were not considered to be real people until they were over the age of three. Therefore, researchers haven't found the remains of infants in graveyards, but only of the children who were old enough to be buried in graveyards. These children were often adorned with heavy jewelry, which was supposed to keep evil spirits away. The children had to wear more jewelry because due to their small size it was believed that it would be easier for spirts to take them away.

Adults also wore certain pieces of jewelry to protect themselves from certain spirits. Of course, they also carried weapons, but the weapons would have specific drawings of people and animals that were said to be protective. This artwork was done in the traditional Celtic style that you still see today.

In their religious practice, Celtic people showed close ties to nature and, in various rituals, used natural elements. Many of the deities related to natural things like the seasons, the sky, wind, or rain. They believed that natural things like plants had spirits and that some would be dangerous. These "dangers" appear in some of the folklore that was created, particularly in Irish folklore.

The Celtic religion also had rules about sovereigns. The health of the king would reflect the health of the country as a whole, so there were various rules that the king had to follow to ensure that the tribe stayed healthy. When a king got a scar or lost a limb, he would lose some of his physical perfection, which the Celts believed would impact their wellbeing. Further, mental imperfections could have negative impacts as well. If a king was greedy, for example, the Earth would be greedy too and not give the people good crops.

An interesting facet of the Celts is that women had more ability to make decisions and be leaders in Celtic societies than many other European and Asian societies. This appreciation of women was probably related to the importance that was placed on family life in Celtic culture.

The religious practices of the Celts were an important part of their daily lives, which were connected to magic and superstition. By living as the deities would want, Celts believed that they could better ensure their safety and health, and they believed that going against their religious practices would cause harm to their tribe and personal wellbeing. Thus, led by the druids, Celts carefully followed various religious traditions and rituals.

Celtic Christianity

When the initial Celtic religion fell out of popularity, a new era of Celtic Christianity was ushered in. While Christianity was common across Europe, the Celtic Christians had some unique behaviors that were carried over from religious principles of the past. Even today, people incorporate Celtic traditions into Christianity to retain some of the Celtic traditions that were formerly lost. They do this to connect to their ancestors and their roots.

Initially, when Christianity took over Paganism, the Celts didn't want to lose their identity entirely. Thus, druids would continue to practice many of their rituals, but they would do so under the guise of Christian values. In their stories, gods and goddesses became kings and queens, so many of the myths could continue to exist, only in a unique manner.

In the year 664 AD, the ruler of the Celtic Christians, King Oswiu, decided that he would have his people become Catholics. His wife was Catholic, so the change didn't feel that extreme to him. Thus, many of the practices of the Celtic Christians were swapped out, and there is very little of that initial wave of Celtic Christianity that remains. Primarily, some prayers are left, but little else remains.

Those who practice Celtic Christianity today are primarily people who live in rural places. Most of their practices are not too extreme, but they do things such as celebrate holidays like Easter on different days than the mainstream Catholic church. They often follow the feast days that were followed in the Celtic religion.

There are different denominations and belief systems among modern Celtic Christians, but there are some common threads that many emphasize in their religions. Many people emphasize the divine wonder of nature. They like to get in touch with natural elements. While they still do not let women be priests, they are willing to allow them some leadership roles within the church. Additionally, they have the unique view that there shouldn't be a divide between sacred things and profane things. What happens within and without church should be merged and should not be looked at separately. They also believe in the power of certain geographical locations. For example, they believe in "thin places." Thin places are locations that the druids believed allowed humans a better view of the world of spirits. Celtic Christians have marked these locations as sacred and use them as places of worship. Celtic Christians also love saints that are seen as especially Celtic such as St. Patrick, St. Brigid, and St. Columba. Further, they love to incorporate both art and music into their religious practices, and utilize Anam Chara, which means "soul friend". Finally, they are a welcoming group that meets in small places and allows anyone to join and keeps a tribal spirit.

The Celtic Christians believe in thresholds. As mentioned in the thin places, they believe that certain places have less of a divide between the human world and the otherworld. They not only believe that certain places have a better connection to the afterlife, but they also believe that certain times of day may have different spiritual properties. They also believe in the power of dreams, and they respect dreams as a sign of something more.

Another important facet of their religion is appreciating daily moments. They like to look at even monotonous moments as a blessing. Thus, they appreciate even the little moments. They see those moments as opportunities for spiritual growth and grace.

In general, Celtic Christianity is more focused on how they practice their faith rather than being rigid in theology like Roman Christianity is. Relatedly, some of the practices of the Celtic Christians may be viewed as heretical by those who are not part of the religion. There are no firm rules for how to be a Celtic Christian, so different members may practice different ways, and the church accepts that. The main goal is to worship God without having to follow Roman Catholic practices to the letter of the law. This allows more opportunity for expression. The group of Celtic Christians that exist today is small, but the religion does live on.

Beyond just the religion itself, Celtic beliefs can be incorporated into the mainstream Catholic or Christian faith. Christianity doesn't have to be distinct from the Celtic religion. They can exist harmoniously, and those who have Celtic origins can embrace those origins while still maintaining their Christian beliefs.

Importance of Other Beings

In the polytheistic Celtic religions of the past, beings beyond just humans or one god were important. They believed in a whole collection of beings that they drove their inspiration from, and they used these beings for inspiration and guidance in their daily lives.

The religion of Celts encompassed far more than just humans. Every part of the universe, both natural and supernatural, was important to the Celts. They included the spirits and needs of much more than themselves into their religious practices. Everything was interconnected, and they needed to acknowledge that interconnectivity to find earthly balance. Thus, many of their rituals and acts of sacrifice were centered around that philosophy.

To the Celts, the whole world was a living thing. They believed that everything in nature has a spirit, and thus, they had certain rules about how they could react around certain things and what the purposes of such things were. Even rocks were considered spirited. Depending on the object, things could have either good, bad, or neutral spirits. Thus, there were a lot of complex, nuanced religious connotations related to even simple natural things.

Many Celts believed in supernatural beings and could be superstitious. Thus, creatures like fairies were considered to have roles in the natural world, and these creatures play parts in many of the Celtic legends. Further, animals and plants had sacred natures of their own, and because they too were said to have spirits, they were treated in unique ways, and they often became part of the myths.

Rituals

Rituals are an important part of any religion, and accordingly, the Celts had various rituals that differed based on the tribe that was practicing. We have limited knowledge of the extent of these rituals, but we know some of the main rituals that were the driving forces behind Celtic religious life. These rituals were practiced in hopes that by completing them, the gods would look favorably upon the Celtic people. Thus, they felt an urgent need to complete these tasks, even if they seem superstitious to us.

Healing Rituals were common because the Celts believed that everything originated in the Otherworld, and thus, they could heal people and protect themselves by appealing to deities. When bad things happened, they believed it was because of instability in the Otherworld, so to fix the problems, they had to try to find a balance between the natural world and the Otherworld. To accomplish healing, therefore, they would combine elements like water, herbs, and other natural items with icons, stories, appeals to gods, music, and other rituals.

The Celtic people also had plant rituals. They would have tree rituals because they believed that trees had healing and magical qualities. Druids would often use flowers in ceremonies, including sacrificial ceremonies. They'd also consume the plants in drinks that they would make, which they considered sacred. These drinks would be made of plants like mead and dandelion. These drinks were said to make the people healthier and would bring happiness to the tribe. Certain plants would also be used for clothing in rituals. Whether people wore clothes and what kind of clothes they wore would vary based on the ritual, and wearing the right clothes could improve rituals.

The Temple Unroofing ritual was a yearly act done primarily by the French Celts. The people would take off the roof of their temple, and then in just one day, they would rebuild the roof. It's a strange ritual, but it is one of the most intriguing.

Sacrifices

Among all the rituals of pagan religions, sacrifices are rituals that are the most scandalous, intriguing, and terrifying part of these religions. While the extent of the sacrifices is unknown, the Celtic people in early times certainly did feel the need to make sacrifices for certain celebrations, and also to avoid bad things happening to them. These sacrifices were not seen as immoral though they certainly would be by today's standards. Julius Caesar found many of the Celtic sacrifice rituals to be strange or barbaric, and he scorned the Celts for that reason.

Sacrifices were one of the major rituals of the Celtic religion. These ritual sacrifices were meant to satisfy the gods and bring good fortune to the Celtic people. As in other cultures, these sacrifices were seen as needed. The Celts would make both animal and human sacrifices to the gods, which would often be done in brutal manners that would probably resemble torture to you. Yet, these grievous acts were a normal part of the Celtic religion. Sacrifices would be made for various reasons that included crime, injury, or simply to appease the gods when bad things happened.

Some people were sacrificed because they had taken another person's life unjustly; thus, by taking a life, the balance must be created by taking away the life of the killer, too. Druids would determine this justice. When their society as a whole would engage in war, they would also make sacrifices to please the gods. After a victory in war, sacrifices would be made, or after a massive loss, sacrifices would also be made. Further, if there was disease running rampant, that would be another reason to sacrifice a human to please the gods. Sometimes, animal sacrifices would do, but in many Celtic cultures, human sacrifices would be used when issues were incredibly serious.

Those who were sacrificed were often slaves, but valued members of Celtic populations would also sometimes be chosen, especially those of lower classes.

The Celts of Gaul had some of the highest rates of human sacrifice among any early religion. They used human and animal sacrifices for a variety of reasons. Not only did the Celtic people sacrifice ordinary people, but evidence from recovered bodies shows that they would even sacrifice their own kings in their rituals. Kings were held to high standards in Celtic culture, so those kings would be sacrificed if it was considered to be for the greater good.

For some human sacrifices, they would use three methods of dying at once. Rarely were sacrifices done quickly and easily. Most of the time, the deaths were brutal. It was common for the Celts to put victims through three different phases. These three-phased deaths are supported by stories such as that of Merlin. For Celtic people, three was a lucky number, so they'd often choose a combination of three death methods to appease the gods because their gods liked distinct manners of death. They could stab a man, hang him, and burn him and that would appease more of the gods because the three methods make it count for three sacrifices.

Head hunts were also used as a method of human sacrifice. During these hunts, warriors would hang the head of the enemy on something sharp and then ride home with the heads. They would then place the heads around the village in a way that was related partially, but not fully, to religion. While there were some religious undertones to headhunting, for the most part, it was just a brutal act.

In Britain, human sacrifice continued until the year 77 AD. Thus, human sacrifice has a long history in Celtic culture, but at the same time, Celts have been distant from those principles for an extensive amount of time, and many Celtic cultures lasted years after all human sacrifice had ceased. Beyond human sacrifice, Celtic cultures used animal sacrifice, which endured for longer.

Animals were sacrificed often to please the gods and to appeal for good fortune. Different animals, like cows, sheep, and goats, would be sacrificed to different gods. When captured from enemies, animals would be sacrificed to war gods. Sometimes, dogs would be sacrificed, and flowers would be placed on their heads. The animals were killed in a variety of ways, some more gruesome than others. Some would be burned, and the remains would be poured on the rest of the herd. Sometimes, bodies were put into the ocean.

Sacrifices are seen as repulsive and illegal in cultures today, but for the Celts, they were just a part of life. They believed that by making the sacrifices, they would improve their luck, ensure that they had good weather conditions, and that they would avoid facing famine, among other issues that were common at the time.

Temples

While early religions didn't have the kinds of temples that you would envision today, the Celts still had a place where they would carry our rituals and have images of gods. It is there that the druids would do some of their work. Temples would be created to hold altars and be surrounded by trees that the people would mark with blood, and they would shape the trunks of trees into various gods or the symbols of gods. Many of these temples were referred to as sacred groves. As society made advancements, these temples became fancier places of worship but maintained many of the same qualities. Some temples would have artifacts like skulls or goods that had been won during battle, which would be given to the gods.

Some people theorize that stone circles like Stonehenge are the remains of Celtic temples, but those are Neolithic according to current research, and many of those circles happened shortly before the Celtic people arose. So, while those sites are interesting, they are unlikely to be Celtic.

On altars in the temples, there would be many goods they won as well as other offerings such as human or animal sacrifices.

Blood would often be dripped on these altars, and generally, the altars would be hidden behind large mounds of dirt.

For iconography, they would craft crude shapes out of tree trunks or use stones to create images, which would honor various entities. Stones would primarily be used for graves, but they occasionally had other purposes as well. For example, they would use them as "boundaries" between the gods.

The temples and how they were decorated were an important part of the Celtic religion. While the temples were fairly sparse, they were still important centers for religious festivals and other rituals.

Main Festivals

In any culture, celebrations show a lot about what is important to that culture and what they most highly value. The Celts did not have too many festivals, but the ones they did have were incredibly elaborate, and some of them are still practiced by people, even now. You may even be familiar with some of them!

The Celts had four main days that they celebrated as holidays, which occur at a regimented pace. While they only had two seasons in their calendar, the dates of the holidays are associated with the four seasons that we know today. For the Celts, they would associate the holidays with growing seasons.

They would hope for good agricultural fortune and gather as communities to celebrate these festivals. Celtic people viewed time as a cycle rather than a line, so the festivals marked the point where they were in that recurring cycle of life. As a result, they would begin their festivals in the evening rather than in the mornings.

January 31 to February 1 is a festival called Imbolc, which is a spring festival to celebrate lambs being born. During this festival, people would eat lamb tails, and women would celebrate the goddess Brigid as a maiden. In some places today, on this day, people will dress a bag of oats in women's clothing and put it out with a club to acknowledge the Celtic roots of Imbolc and a ritual that many ancient Celts participated in. On this day, people often made large bonfires to honor Brigid. This holiday would later become the feast day of the Christian St. Brigid, who is said to be the Christian version of the goddess.

April 30 to May 1 is a festival called Beltain. This festival was related to fire, and they would have huge bonfires during this time. They'd also play various board games, so it was an incredibly fun and lighthearted festival. The focus of this festival is having plenty and being fertile, both concerning people and the land. Cows were released from their confinements and allowed to roam again at this time, and both humans and cows would begin to start their reproductive processes. During this time, people were also allowed to divorce spouses. This festival was commonly associated with the god Belenos, and was a time for ritual cleansing.

Beginning on August 31st, Lughnasadh was a festival that could last for weeks. It is a festival held to honor the god Lugh. Because Lugh was a skilled god, they would hold competitions during this holiday. One of the biggest competitions that they had was horse racing. When they weren't racing the horses, they were allowed to swap their horses for other horses.

October 31st to November 1st is the final festival that the Celts celebrated, and it occurred as what is now known as Halloween. This festival was called Samhain. This festival marks the start of winter and the end of the harvest time. The year generally began with this season. During this occasion, it was thought that the veil between life and death was so thin that the dead could pass through it from the Otherworld. At this time, all battle was halted until May, and the cattle were brought into enclosures for winter. On this day, the Celts were said to have put skulls outside their houses.

These festivals were important occasions for Celts. During these times, they could have little breaks from their ordinary, difficult lives. Festivals celebrated the changing of the seasons and the various gods who were sacred to the Celts. While the festivals represented various things, they all were done in the hope that the future would be favorable to them.

Death

Death rituals are common across all cultures. Many of these rituals include burials and tombstones to mark where the dead are. Little is known about the rituals of the Celts, but archeologists have made educated guesses on some of their main death rituals.

While the celts didn't believe that people would live on Earth forever, they did believe in people living on after burial, as many other religions believe. Celts believed that there was an afterlife, and that people would never truly die and would instead move on to another world. The move to the afterlife did not seem connected to good or bad deeds like it was when Christians began taking over. Some Celtic people would be buried with a prized possession of theirs. Others seem to have been cremated due to a lack of burial grounds. Celtic people in Gaul were buried with food, weapons, and other treasures so that they'd be ready for the afterlife.

Archaeologists have found large animal bones near burial sites, indicating that Celts likely had huge feasts when someone died, and they would often drink their version of beer, or when the person who died was wealthier, they would sometimes drink wine. Even among poorer people, it is estimated that Celts had some sort of celebration for the lost life, centered around food and drink.

While the exact death rituals of the Celtic people of the past are widely unknown, we do know that the Celtics took death seriously and that a person's death marked a passage into a new life of some sort. We also know that, to some extent, people's lives were celebrated through feasts held at the gravesite.

Chapter 4: Celtic Deities and Creatures

The Power of Deities and Creatures

Deities were vital to the culture of Celtic people. They used stories of the gods to guide their decisions and to ask for what they wanted and needed. Families passed down stories of the gods to teach their children about the Celtic faith that was shared for many generations. These stories were predominately told rather than written down.

Not only were deities important, but so were other mythological creatures that had stories of their own, and often interacted with humans and the deities alike. These creatures often had magical properties, and many of them still are talked about today.

Unfortunately, because many of these stories relied on oral tradition, much of the lore behind the deities were not written down. Thus, there's some mystery about the true nature of deities and other mythical creatures. Even after Christianity took over, a good amount of Celtic beliefs have been preserved to feed our interest. Archeologists and historians have been able to fill in some of the gaps.

The Celtic deities vary across cultures, but the most important or fascinating ones have been listed here for your convenience. Many have similarities, but they each have unique properties that appealed to the people who worshipped them. If you're a lover of other types of mythologies, you may be able to see overlap, and it can be fun to look at these mythological entities through a comparative lens.

Terminology

You only have to know a couple of main terms to understand the deities and myths that are important in Celtic religion. While many terms could be thrown in, I've condensed them to the ones that are vital to understanding the content in this book, so as to not complicate matters.

Triple Goddesses

The triple goddesses are composed of the maiden, mother, and the crone figures, all in one deity. Three separate goddesses may make up the parts of this deity, or it may be made up of just one goddess. The Maiden is the young woman, the mother is the middle-aged woman, and the crone is the old woman. These three goddesses represent the different life stages of women. While the Celtic people wouldn't have classified the goddesses this way, it is an archetype that has been created by scholars to explain the function of certain goddesses. The maiden is virginal and youthful while the mother is fertile and nurturing, and the crone is considered a hag who is full of wisdom. These three types often classify goddesses, and some goddesses can appear in multiple forms. Altogether, these three types can make a triple goddess who is both fully the three distinct goddesses, while still be her own full entity.

Mabinogion

These are stories that were published in Britain around the twelfth century. It is a compilation that includes many of the first written versions of folktales; thus, making it an important source for information about classic Celtic stories. The *Four Branches of the Mabinogi* contains an extensive amount of Celtic mythology, and it can still be read today. There are various branches of this book that capture different stories in each portion. This is just one of the various story anthologies that have been published about Celtic myth, but it is one of the most prevalent and one of the most studied.

Tuatha De Danann

This term refers to a tribe of gods that is considered to be the main Irish Celtic figures. It means the "people of Danu," referring to the goddess who serves as a mother figure. These deities reside in the Otherworld, and they can appear in various forms, sometimes even as animals. Some are witches, and some are shapeshifters. They are all-powerful forces who have some kind of influence on the natural world. Many stories of this group were eventually written down by Christian monks, so some information may have been skewed in that time. In Christian writings, the characters are often referred to as kings and queens rather than as gods and goddesses. This group includes the main god, the Dagda, Danu (AKA Anu), Lugh, Brigid, Morrigan, Aengus, Mannanan, Nuada, Cecht, Dian, and Goibniu. These gods are some of the ones who have the most research on them because they were among the gods that were written about.

Tain Bo Cualinge

This is an Irish epic that has been compared to the Illiad. It is important to mythology because it includes mythological figures from the Celtic canon. It is one of the main sources of Celtic mythology, and it is an important part of Irish culture that is still studied presently.

The Ulster Cycle

The Ulster Cycle is a collection of Irish stories that includes many of the myths that involve the area of Ulster. It is an ancient work that contains first-century stories that were gathered from oral retellings of those stories. They were written from the eighth to eleventh centuries, and the collection was finally published in the twelfth century. The collection focuses on the lives of King Conchobar and those close to him, and it includes Queen Medb and Cu Chulainn as well as Lug. In this work, the gods are referred to as royalty or warriors rather than as deities. They were referred to as such because of the era in which they were recorded. Most of these stories are written succinctly, and depict adventure amid normal circumstances, so they focus on cattle raids and basic adventures of the like. Poets like William Butler Yeats have retold these stories in the twentieth century. *The Cattle Raid of Cooley* is the longest work in the collection, but many famous stories are included.

Gods and Goddesses

Aengus

Aengus was an Irish, shapeshifting god who was associated with love and poems and was married to Caer Ibormeith, who was the woman of his dreams (a story that you'll learn more about later). He was referred to as the "Young One" because of his young age in the myths. His mother was the goddess Boann, and his father was Dagda. Like his father, Aengus could be incredibly beguiling. He was known for using music and poems to woo ladies, motivate royalty, and sway his enemies. He often used his skills to manipulate situations. His powers also included the ability to bring people back from the dead due to his youthfulness. While he could breathe life into people, sometimes his resurrections would be short-lived. He loved birds, and accordingly, he could turn kisses into birds. His weapon collections included two spears, as well as two swords. He also used his trusty harp to lure people in and make them do as he wanted. He had multiple siblings, including Midir, Brigid, and Cermait.

Anu

Anu, also known as Danu, was an Irish goddess who represented the source of all life and was a mother figure of the gods. She was the Earth goddess and was associated with the land as well as bodies of water. Like most goddesses, she was depicted as beautiful, but more than that, she represented fertility and was said to bring a good harvest. Celts viewed bees as her messengers, and people worshipped her so that they would have bountiful supplies of food. Some influence of her lore still lingers, and there is a mountain area that is called Paps of Anu after this Earth goddess. Some considered her the most powerful of all Irish goddesses.

Arianrhod

Arianrhod was the goddess of celestial bodies, and her name means silver wheel. She was sometimes known as Margause or Margawse. A pale-skinned goddess represented by a sow and a cauldron, she was often found around other women, but she was also liberal with her sexual behaviors and loved to have affairs with mermen. She was in charge of life's tapestry, as part of her connection to spinning and weaving. Like many deities, she could be deceptive and was good at magic, which she used to her advantage several times. She was also the victim of other gods' trickery, which resulted in her birthing her twins.

Arwan

Arwan, a primarily Welsh deity, was a king of the underworld, and thus, had some darker associations, but he was known for wanting to give justice in the underworld and provided rightful punishments. Good at hunting and shapeshifting, he used his skills to rule over Annwn, which was an otherworld, or place of afterlife. Annwn never had a shortage of food, and it promised eternal happiness and youth. Annwn is similar to the later Christian idea of heaven. While Arwan was the ruler of paradise, as Christians tried to speak against mythology, he became the lord of a darker otherworld that people went to when they did not go to Christianity's Heaven. While there isn't a whole lot of detail about Arwan's family life, he is known to have a beloved wife, Annwn. He lives on through pop culture today, including through the game Dungeons and Dragons.

Badb

As the goddess of war, Badb was not one you'd want to anger. Her name meant crow. She was known as a crone, or an older woman, who brought death during the war. She was one of the three goddesses who made up Morrigan, her being the crone version of Morrigan, but she would sometimes take on a younger form. Fittingly, she married the god of war, Neit, who her sister also happened to be married to, making for a complex family dynamic. As Morrigan, she was the wife of Dagda as well, showing the complex familial dynamics that many gods and goddesses had.

Belenus

As one of the oldest and most common Celtic gods, Belenus was often viewed as the Celtic version of the Apollo, but the evidence doesn't support the claim that he was a sun god because the Celts used the sun as a religious symbol more than as something to worship. Rather, he seems to be more closely linked to cattle and horses. He also has some links to healing or light, as his name means "bright one." He was often found in Celtic areas in modern-day Italy, Switzerland, France, or Austria. Being so old, the research on him is limited, but at the time of worship, he was a profound god in some Celtic regions.

Belisama

Belisama was a goddess mostly found in the Gaul (today's France) region as well as Britain. She was a powerful goddess who was associated with rivers and fire. Like Belenus, the information we have about her exact powers are limited because of how much has been lost, but she has also been associated as an Apollo sort of goddess. Researchers have concluded that she was a popular goddess and that she was often worshipped before battles, but much of her impact was wiped away as the Roman empire strived to replace Celtic mythology with their own mythology.

Blodeuwedd

Blodeuwedd was a Welsh goddess who was represented by both flowers and owls. Created by magicians, she was created to marry Lleu Llaw Gyffes (more on that later). She was associated with hope, relationships, and charity, and was said to have a face of flowers. When she cheated on her husband, she was said to have been turned into an owl, which she was forced to continue being, losing her previous beauty. She represents how easily trust in relationships can be broken. She eternally pines for her lost love because she went from being in an enriching relationship, to being a lone creature who only came out at night. Through her painful experiences, she learned to be wise and imparted her wisdom on those who learned of her story.

Brigid

Brigid was an Irish goddess who was the daughter of the Dagda, and who married Bres. She is often seen as the goddess of spring and is therefore associated with fertility and healing. She also was a tough goddess as she was linked to martial arts and smithcraft. Despite her toughness, she was also known for her poetry. She is often associated with the Christian Saint Brigid, who has a feast day at the start of spring and represents many similar notions as the Celtic goddess. Saint Brigid's feast day is shared with Brigid's feast day on February 1st, which was called Imbolc. She is mostly seen as a mother or sometimes as a maiden, but because she has multiple forms, she may have been a triple goddess. She was a master of many crafts, and therefore, was one of the most popular Celtic goddesses. While she was in charge of summer, Cailleach was in charge of winter.

Britania

Britania was a British goddess who would be used to represent the British empire. She had connections to Minerva, a war goddess. She was first referred to in the second century in Britain. She is divine and is associated with lunar cycles and doing magic with rabbits. Not much else is known about her, but she is associated with British power.

Cailleach

Cailleach was often called the Queen of Winter, or the Veiled one. She was worshipped in various Celtic areas such as Scotland, Ireland, and the Isle of Man. She was responsible for how brutal, or mild winter would be and was in charge of the wind. She is considered an old woman figure, and her name has become a Gaelic word that means old woman. She has been an inspiration for many poets because of how prominent she was.

She was also connected to people's ability to have sovereignty. To rule over a country, sovereigns would first have to ask her to agree to them ruling over that area. As the winter goddess, she also ruled over grain, which was a food that would help people survive the long winter months. As a hag figure, it's no wonder that she outlived her spouses and her children. She was often said to have had immortality.

Ceridwen

As a white witch, Ceridwen was a Welsh goddess who could shapeshift and was filled with wisdom. She is among the most powerful of all the Celtic witches, and she possesses 'Awen', which is the power of three things— prophecy, poetic wisdom, and inspiration. Using her cauldron, she can further her magical skills. Part of her powers also come from a throne that is filled with magic. As a white witch, her powers were used for good, and much of the time, her acts were selfless, but there were occasions when she did use her powers for selfish reasons. With a bit of a temper when things didn't go her way, she could wander from her usual goodness sometimes, but she always found her way back to righteousness and continued to use her magic for good in the end.

Cermait

Cermait was an Irish god who was the son of the Dagda. He was killed after he had an affair with another man's wife. Upon his killing, his father cried bloody tears for him and was able to bring Cermait back to life. He had three sons who would get revenge for his death, and he was also related to Aengus and Brigid.

Cernunnos

Cernunnos was another one of the gods whose history is a bit cloudy because of lost information, but from what we know, he was a Gaelic god who ruled over beasts and other untamed things. He had the power to take foes and bring them together, which could be used to restore peace to the world. He was used in many Gaelic regions, and his name means horned one. He often is portrayed as himself having horns, as well as a beard, and he commonly wore a Celtic necklace called a torc. In the nineteenth century, people began bringing him back into consciousness and using him in literature.

Clíodhna

Clíodhna was an Irish goddess known as the goddess of beauty and love, but she was also known as the queen of the banshees. Generally, she was portrayed as having three birds around her who would cure people with their songs. When people heard the birds' music, they would fall asleep and wake up free from their ailments. She gave up her life in paradise to be with a mortal man she loved. She was later taken away by a wave when her lover went hunting, and in legend, strong waves in Ireland were known as her wave.

Creiddylad

Creiddylad was a Welsh goddess who represented flowers as well as love. Celts called her the May Queen, and she sought to ease instability and chaos. As one of the most peaceful goddesses, she showed the power of perseverance and how it leads to calmness. Another lesson she taught was that to love oneself was a crucial part of loving others, because taking care of yourself gives you the mental clarity and physical ability to care for others. She was supposed to be married to a man who she loved, but then she was kidnapped. Her betrothed fought for her freedom, but in doing so he committed atrocious acts, so he was then not permitted to marry Creiddylad. As a result, each May, two men would have to fight for her hand perpetually, but she would remain unmarried. While not wed, she represented fertility.

Cu Chulainn

Cu Chulainn is one of the most well-known Irish figures in mythology. He was a warrior who became an expert at war and could challenge multiple adversaries at once. He killed many people, and he had immense strength and stamina. He would get enraged during wars and would end up killing anyone who was in his way. While his lineage is not precisely clear, he is known to be the descendent of gods, and despite being born in Dundalk, he considered Ulster his home.

The Dagda

The Dagda is an important god in Irish Celtic mythology. He was the Chief of the Tuatha De Danann, and is portrayed as a father figure, and a king. The Dagda, also known as the 'good god', was highly skillful with a club, and was known for his great wisdom. He wielded a club of life and death, a harp that could control both the seasons and men alike, and a cauldron of plenty. He had many children, and many lovers. He was a powerful god, and is associated with fertility, agriculture, life, and death.

Epona

Epona was a goddess of horses, and she was found in Gaul and Germany. Interestingly, she was also worshipped in Rome, which was unusual, and they considered her the goddess of cavalry because of her connections to horses. Thus, her influence went far beyond normal Celtic areas. In Celtic areas, she was said to keep horses safe, and she also protected donkeys and ponies, but as Rome overtook places like Gaul, she became more of a warrior goddess. She was part of the imperial cult. Because of her Roman connection, she was in many pieces of classic Roman art. She also has been used in British art and literature. She is still worshipped today by some believers.

Flidais

Flidais was a goddess, who like Anu, was associated with the Earth. She is a Mother Earth figure, who was commonly found in parts of Ireland. She mothered several of the gods and goddesses that were associated with Earth and agriculture. Flidais was unique in that she represented the wildness and the domesticity of humanity, merging the natural and cultural tendencies of life. She guarded over forest animals, and those that are domesticated alike, again showing her role in both the home and in nature. She was a nurturer, and beyond that, she was a shapeshifter who could heal and use magic.

Gwydion

Gwydion was a Welsh god who can be found in the *Fourth Branch of Mabinogi* as well as some other writings that were written after the fact. He was mischievous and often used his power to trick others. He was able to change other beings into other things using his magic. He was known for his skills as a warrior because of his ability to take down a powerful Welsh lord quickly. He would also make flowers into women. Despite his mischief, Gwydion stood by those he cared about, such as his nephew, Lleu. He served as a wise confidant to his nephew.

Thus, his role in Welsh mythology is similar to the role of Dagda in Irish mythology, who was the adviser to several kings, including Lugh. Gwydion lives on even now, and you can find him in modern works of literature such as Neil Gaiman's *American Gods*.

Herne the Hunter

Herne the Hunter was a ghost god that would wader the woods of the English countryside. He lives on because of his inclusion in Shakespeare's *The Merry Wives of Windsor,* but it has been speculated that he appeared long before Shakespeare in the Celtic canon. He was known to walk around with shackles on, and he and stayed near a tree named Herne's Oak. He was not a nice mythological creature and scared away animals or humans with his ghoulishness. According to legend, he had antlers on a hood that was made from deerskin. He had the power to make things rot. If he touched a tree, he could make it die. He represented the destruction of the natural world. Whenever people would see Herne, it was assumed that there was going to be a devastating event in the nation, or that a large number of people were going to die. In any case, he was a haunting figure who didn't represent anything good.

Lugh

Lugh was known as the god of royalty and was advised by the Dagda on several occasions. He had a spear made of lightning called the Assal. He was good at crafting all items and was a fierce soldier who was unstoppable when he held his spear. A member of the Tuatha De Danann, this Irish god represented strength and power. He was a well-rounded god who lived up to his lofty status as the god of all kings. He was also known as being a fair judge, but that doesn't mean he wasn't a cunning adversary. When he needed to, he was willing to break the rules to win against an opponent. He had many wives, which resulted in him having several children, but most notably, he was also the father of the esteemed Cú Chulainn, who was one of the greatest Irish heroes in mythology.

Macha

Macha was an Irish goddess who was married to Crunniuc. She was the goddess of war, and she was considered to be part of the triple goddess, Morrigan. Of Morrigan, she was considered to be the raven of the trio because the Morrigan would often appear as birds when going to battle. She was associated with horses, because of a race she ran at the king's behest. Rumor had it that she could run faster than any horse, so she engaged in a race with the king's horses. She was pregnant, but the king would not let her stop the race so that she could give birth, and she had to finish the race, which she won. Some legends say that she died in childbirth and that she cursed men to be in pain. Macha represented fertility as well as motherhood. She often liked to ease people's suffering.

Medb

Medb was a goddess who was the Queen of Connacht. She was an incredibly sexual, Irish goddess who disagreed with Cú Chulainn after an argument with her once husband, Conchobar. She was known for having both emotional and physical strength that rivaled that of the men in her life. She was strong-willed and expected the men in her life to treat her with dignity. She had numerous lovers because she was beautiful and alluring. She was content with her promiscuity and enjoyed her power. Some say that she inspired Queen Mab in Shakespeare's famous play, *Romeo and Juliet*. Given Shakespeare's love for mythology, that wouldn't be a surprise.

Merlin

Merlin was known for his role in Arthurian legend, which has long been told and retold, but he was also a prominent part of Celtic legend, sometimes called Myrddin. He was the god of the druids in Welsh and English tales. Britain was actually once referred to as Myrddin's Enclosure, showing the importance of this mythical figure. He was a great sorcerer in Celtic myth and very powerful, but in Arthurian tales, Merlin, and the other gods, became simply slightly magical kings, queens, and knights. He was not a major player in Celtic mythology, but because of his lasting impact through newer myths, he is a profound part of the Celtic canon, and his character holds much intrigue even now.

Midir

Midir was a lesser-known god in the Tuatha de Danann, and he was said to have been the god who created the smaller bodies of water in the Irish countryside. He was predominantly featured in a story about him and his lover, a fairy named Etain. Etain was then turned into a butterfly and blown far away by the wind. She died, and she was reborn as a princess. She grew up and had married the Irish king by the time Midir found her again. To win over Etain, Midir challenged her husband to a game of chess, and won. Accordingly, he ended up winning a kiss with Etain. When he went to kiss her, he was intimidated by the king's guards, but he broke through and got Etain for himself. The King of the Fairies then appeared and told Etain's husband that if he was able to choose Etain from a lineup of fifty women who looked just like her that he could have his wife back. The legends are conflicting, with some of them saying that he chose the wrong woman while in others, he chose the right one.

The Morrigan

The Morrigan was a triple goddess, who was often associated with birds and battle. She was part of the Tuatha de Danann, and she was supposedly married to the Dagda, and she was made of three goddesses: Badb, Macha, and Neiman. She was portrayed as youthful with dark, long hair. She could be quite seductive and often wore black clothing or cloaks. As a shapeshifter, she could often be seen as birds like crows or ravens. She could easily handle opponents and was feared by many. She was willing to kill her adversaries as needed and could manipulate them to get her way. She was one of the most notable of all the Irish goddesses.

Neiman

Neiman was the third goddess to make up the Morrigan. Not too much was written about Neiman beyond her role as part of the Morrigan. However, she does show up in some Irish myths. She was part of the Tuatha de Danann, so she is one of the important Irish deities.

Neit

Neit was married to Neiman, but he was also married to another part of the Morrigan, Badb. He was an Irish war god who died in battle. He was well respected by soldiers and a member of the Tuatha de Danann. The Dagda was his nephew. He doesn't show up too much in Celtic mythology, but he was connected to many of the prominent figures. Sometimes, he was referred to as Neto, and in those cases, he was linked to the Roman gods Apollo and Mars.

Nuada

Nuada was a member of the Tuatha de Danann. He was the first king of this group, and he was known for his silver prosthetic hand. He was also known for his honesty and fairness, and he was good at both hunting and fishing. Unlike many of the other gods, he obeyed the rules that he made for others, even when they made his life harder. His weapon was a sword that no one could defeat, which was one of four artifacts of the Tuatha de Danann. He lost his kingship because of trickery by the Dagda. He was married to Boann, who he had no children with and would later divorce. All in all, he was a strong leader, and one of the most judicious of all the gods.

Ogma

Ogma was another member of the Tuatha De Danann, and he was a god of language and speech. He was the son of the Dagda and Anu. He was a talented talker, and no one could make better speeches than him. He was also excellent at poetry, and in general, he was good with words, so he could use his oratory skills to get people on his side, which made him incredibly convincing. He is sometimes associated with the god Ogmios, who is a Gaelic god. He's strongly linked with the gods Lugh and the Dagda, who he helps in the story of the Dagda's harp.

Taranis

Taranis was the god of thunder and storms, and he was found across Celtic cultures. There aren't many lasting details about this god, but he had full control of storms, which induced fear in people. While powerful, he was a protector and would protect other gods. The Romans reported that he was one of the gods who people gave human sacrifices too. While he used a lightning bolt as a weapon, his main symbol, and one of the most prominent Celtic symbols, was a wheel, which represented how an unexpected storm could incapacitate humans, as well as representing motion.

White Lady

The White Lady was a goddess/being that is found in all Celtic cultures and most cultures in general. She was considered in some myths to be the goddess of devastation and mortality, and she was considered a crone. She was sometimes called the Queen of the dead. Sometimes, she was talked about more like a ghost story and was referred to as Y Ladi Wen or Dynes Mewn Gwyn. She was used to scare children into behaving well and to warn them not to be greedy. It is said that when people talked to this lady in white that she would offer gold. Sometimes, she asked for help in exchange for a prize. In any case, she was vengeful and attacked people for being greedy and taking her gold.

Fairies

Fairies are one of the most important races in Celtic supernatural myth. They still captivate people's imaginations, which makes them one of the most enduring parts of Celtic myths. Much of how people perceive fairies now is different than it once was. In Celtic times, types of fairies were diverse, and only some of them looked like the pretty little pixies we think of today.

Celtic fairies were sometimes known as Aos Sí. They are occasionally referred to as Fae or faeries as well. Sometimes, they were said to live in a world of their own while other times they lived within the Earth in fairy mounds. They can be found in written versions of the Tuatha De Danann. They are portrayed in a variety of ways. In modern times, they are viewed as elegant, tiny, and cute, but that was not always the case. In some legends, they are troll-like and ugly, while in others, they are angelic. In all lore, they are winged or magical creatures. There are several types of fairies that each have unique characteristics.

Generally, in Celtic myths, fairies have been forced to hide themselves away from society because of an invasive force. In Irish legend, they live on a magical island called Tir Na Nog. They are both known to be mischievous, but also to be caring and aim to heal people with their magic. Some would even teach their abilities to humans. People would often leave treats like chocolate, milk, or nice stones to appease the fairies and stop them from causing trouble. Certain items like four-leaf clovers, herbs, and bells are said to displease the fairies.

While sometimes good-natured to humans, many tales talk about fairies stealing babies and other humans and swapping them for changelings. Further, they are known for using a currency called fairy gold, which looks like gold, but once the debt has been paid, it turns into a cookie or a similarly unhelpful item. Time in the fairy world is said to go more quickly, and when humans eat fairy food in the fairy world, they will become trapped, as legend has it. Fairies also possess many plants and mounds, and if someone were to hurt those areas, the fairies would punish them.

Fairies have long been an essential part of Celtic folklore, and their role in early times established them as an important mythical creature. These mischievous and sometimes loving beings are today portrayed as cute, little, girlish things that are nice but free-spirited; however, past fairies were much more diverse and played an interesting role in Celtic stories. They are one of the most enduring influences of Celtic mythology. There are two main groups of fairies: Seelies and Unseelies.

Seelies

Fairies can be broken up into good and evil fairies. Seelies are fairies that have a higher status than Unseelies. Those who make up Seelie Court are the fairies that probably come to mind when you hear the word. They are gorgeous, and when a human sees them, they can't help but be entranced. Some are ugly, but mostly the beautiful fairies are Seelies. These fairies are kind and compassionate. Love is their chief goal, and they love finding humans who are just as beautiful as they are. They also value youth because it is connected to their beauty. These Seelies, like any fairies, still love to create mischief from time to time, but they are not mean spirited and will not do any real damage to others. In the Tuatha De Danann, these fairies are the good fairies, and the evil Unseelie Court juxtaposes them. Seelie fairies include Leprechauns, Hobgoblins, Selkies, and Brownies.

Unseelies

The Unseelie Court is comprised of the evil fairies. These are not the cute little fairies that you've probably seen in cartoons. They go far beyond just mischievous, and often have cruel intentions. These fairies hate humans and will take every chance to cause destruction and chaos among humans. The ugliness of these fairies' insides often matches their ugly outsides, but some may take on beautiful forms to lure people in. They use their power for harmful purposes and enjoy doing so. They are without honor, and don't take accountability for their actions because they only care about getting what they want. They are selfish and are not concerned with the opinions of other beings. Unseelies include Bogarts and Finfolk.

Bogarts

Bogarts are sometimes associated with the concept of the bogeyman. Like Brownies and Hobgoblins, they can hang around in houses, or they sometimes live outside in marshes, but unlike the more helpful Seelies, they do not help the households or environments they live in. Instead, they terrorize people. They do purposely harmful actions like making items disappear or even hurting family pets. They also have an association with scaring or kidnapping children. If a family tries to escape a Bogart, it will haunt them. Some myths claimed that neglected Brownies or Selkies could become a Bogart, but that is not always the case. Legend says that hanging a horseshoe by the door and sprinkling salt keeps these fairies away from people's homes.

Brownies

Brownies are similar to Hobgoblins, but they are more mischievous and more vengeful. Generally, they are goodhearted, but if they are insulted, they can become petty. They require a gift or milk, and in exchange, they help around a household or on a farm. If they are mistreated, they will leave their households and not return, which happens often because they are sensitive to criticism and mistreatment. They are easily perturbed and get frustrated with lazy people. Sometimes they are portrayed as ghosts of servants who died, but that is not always the case, and often, they are classified as fairies, but in some tales, they are other creatures.

Changeling

Changelings are creatures associated with stories about fairies, who would swap out human children for Changelings so that they could kidnap the mortal babies. Mischievous and evil fairies wreaked havoc on mortals. Changelings are fairies who are placed in the position of the children and would cause trouble with the families that they were placed with. The children would be used for various reasons such as servitude, or sometimes the fairies would merely want affection from the kid. Alternatively, they would take children to seek revenge on humans, or simply to be cruel.

The fairies would kidnap beautiful babies, and before the babies were taken, the children would sometimes become paralyzed or sick, which humans associated with fairies being around. Parents would suspect that a fairy had taken their child, but they would have to treat the Changeling kindly because if they didn't, they worried that the fairies would treat their actual child harshly or kill them.

Knowing that Changelings aren't real makes the myth grimmer because of how those children were treated. Even in the 19th century, some people still believed in Changelings, and one man even killed his wife because he believed that she was a Changeling. When bad things happened to their children, people were quick to associate the issues to fairies rather than accept that their child was deformed or dying. Sadly, Changelings were just normal kids, and they were often mistreated when their parents determined they were Changelings rather than accepting that they were sick or otherwise different than average kids.

Clerichaun

The Clerichaun is a shoemaking fairy that is similar to the Leprechaun, but it is a lesser-known creature. He is known to hang out near places where alcoholic beverages are served, and accordingly, he likes to drink a lot. He prefers to keep to himself, and he is usually alone, so he is considered a solitary fairy rather than a fairy who is part of a troop. He is often described as being tiny, and he is a nuisance, but he is not generally malevolent, so having him around would be a bother but not a nightmare. He does love jokes and pranks, but if he likes a family, he will help them out around the house, so he is considered a Seelie fairy.

Fairy Queen

The Fairy Queen originates from British and Irish folktales. She is often associated with Shakespeare, but her influence predates him. She is said to rule over all the fairies. She has been used since Celtic times in many pieces of literature and movies. Tinker Bell, for example, is a Fairy Queen. Fairy Queens can be seen across cultures but are sometimes known by different names.

Far Darrig

Far Dariig is an Irish fairy whose name comes from the words 'red man' because he wears red clothes. This fairy is a solitary fairy, who lives to play pranks on people, and these pranks are not of the harmless variety. These fairies often play cruel jokes, including swapping babies out for Changelings and are nightmarish figures in Irish lore. Sometimes, these fairies are called rat boys because of how gruesome they are, and because in some legends, they are plump figures with long, thin tails like rats. They are not a type of fairy that you would want to be around and are of course, Unseelies.

Finfolk

Finfolk are unique fairies that often live in water. They are often associated with mermaids, but they do not take the shape of a mermaid. They do have fins on their bodies, though. Finfolk were known to make sleazy deals with human fishermen, and they lived lavish lives under the sea in a paradise known as Finfolkaheem. The women are born looking like mermaids and stay that way until they are older, but when they wed, they lose their beauty if they marry Finfolk men. But, if they marry humans, they can stay beautiful. Finfolk become vengeful when fishermen try to take their fishing areas as their own, and they will put holes in the fishermen's boats while they are out at sea. Many Finfolk will also kidnap humans to marry them, and they possess strong magical abilities.

Gancanagh

Gancanagh is a Scottish and Irish fairy. It is often related to the Incubus, which is a creature that was often associated with sexual assault, but the Celtic version tends to be more mischievous than terrifying compared to the Incubus, and the Scottish version is fairly mild. Gancanagh are handsome and often have dark or red hair, but occasionally, they can be blonde. They use cunning to try to attract partners, but they have selfish intentions. This creature doesn't like long term relationships, so it tends to have many female partners, and it doesn't let them get too close. Women in Celtic times knew to be careful of this creature's charms.

Hobgoblin

Hobgoblins are often portrayed as hairy, small men who live in human houses. They do chores around the house as the family sleeps, so they are good-natured. They work free of charge and only ask to be fed in exchange for their household duties. While they are kind, they are prone to hijinks as mischievous as most other fairies. Their shenanigans can be frustrating, but overall, they want what is best for the households that they live in.

Joint-eater

The Joint-eater fairy is a unique fairy that is invisible and sits next to its victim, eating half of its victim's food as the victim has their meal. While that sounds annoying but doesn't sound too terribly malicious, it gets worse. When a person sleeps, a Joint-eater will slither down their throat and eat half of the food that the host had already consumed. Thus, a person who is being trailed by one of these fairies cannot keep on weight. If a fairy version of a tapeworm exists, this is the fairy. As you can probably guess, it is an Unseelie fairy because of its awful deeds and ugliness.

Leanan Sídhe

This term refers to a beautiful female fairy who finds a handsome human lover and beguiles him into falling in love with her. If the lover of her choosing doesn't take her on as a lover, she then is required to be that man's slave, but once the man agrees to her advances, he cannot escape unless he finds a suitable replacement for himself. She drains the life out of him to maintain her beauty and youth. The men die, and then she must continuously find new lovers to steal the life from. Don't let her beauty be deceiving because she is malicious and sneaky.

Leprechauns

You've surely heard of Leprechauns before, but you may not realize that in folklore, they are commonly referred to as solitary fairies. They often are portrayed as small men with beards, coats, and hats. They are mischievous creatures, but they are good willed. The Leprechauns may like some nice practical jokes, but they don't do permanent harm onto people. Since Celtic times, they have become associated with happiness, pots of gold, cereal, and rainbows. They are also widely used in celebrations of the Christian St. Patrick's Day. Those Leprechauns sure have come a long way!

Pooka

Pooka can be either quite fortunate or quite unlucky, depending on the lore. They are shapeshifters who turn into animals. They are often furry creatures. Some do great harm, but most are simply mischievous. They can't help but cause a little bit of trouble. Many like to terrify people without doing any lasting harm. They'll give humans a scary ride but then return them from where they came from, so they aren't that harmful, but they are terrifying.

Selkie

Selkies are Celtic fairies that resemble seals. They can put their seal skin on and off to change forms. There are male and female selkies. They are both beautiful in their human forms, but the men are particularly alluring. Selkies can be vindictive, and they are incredibly mysterious creatures. They are not as cruel as some of the more malicious fairies, but they are still ones that you wouldn't want to encounter.

Other Creatures

Several other creatures are found in Celtic mythology that are distinct from fairies. Many of these creatures are terrifying monsters, but some of them are not nearly that malicious!

Abhartach

The Abhartach is fundamentally an old, Celtic version of a vampire. In Irish, the word Abhartach means "dwarf," and this creature was referred to as the King of the Dwarves. He was once a living person until he became a blood-sucking creature. The Abhartach was actually the inspiration for the 1897 classic book, *Dracula*. While Dracula was in part inspired by other vampire lore found in Romania, specifically Transylvania, the author, Bram Stoker, was Irish and, therefore, also drew from the Celtic version of the vampire. As the legend goes, there was a King Abhartach who died after falling from a building. He was climbing the estate of the man who Abhartach thought his wife was cheating on him with. Shortly after his death, Abhartach came back to life with a desire to cut people's wrists so that he could drink their blood. Based on this myth, the Celtic vampire stories permeated the culture.

Balor

One of the most powerful Celtic mythical monsters is Balor. Celtic mythology often refers to Balor as the king of the demons. Some myths have him as the god of death, but others refer to him as a straight-up monster. He is said to be a cyclops with just a single gigantic eye. He also only has one single huge leg. With his eye, he is said to be able to kill someone with even just a glance, making people want to steer clear of this evil monster. He was said to be in charge of creatures like the Fomori, who were demons that resided far down in darkest parts of the water. When Balor was killed by his own son, the Formori were left to their own devices, becoming evil sea creatures who hurt humans. Whether you consider him to be a god or just a monster, this creature is one of the worst of the worst.

Banshee

The Banshee is another intimidating and haunting Irish monster that is sometimes associated with the Dullahan. Both of them are said to sometimes share a horse-drawn death cart. The Banshee is one of the most notorious creatures of Irish legend because of how much it has been used in storytelling, even in the modern era. You can find her on TV shows and in books. This is a female monster that foretells death with a shrill wailing sound. If someone were to hear a Banshee outside of their house, they would know that someone in their family was going to die. There are various interpretations of what this creature looked like. Some people said that she was a hideous old woman, while others described her as a gorgeous maiden. Either way, the sound that came out of her was universally horrific. Hearing her cries would only bring bad things upon a family.

Caorthannach

This monster is one of the scariest of them all because it is a fire-spitter, and it has a long history in Ireland, even in times after Catholicism had taken over. In some tales, this monster is the mother of the devil. It is considered to have been kicked out of Ireland for good by St. Patrick. That last part of the legend was inspired by Catholicism when it came into Ireland. Sometimes this creature is called a Caoranach.

Carman

Carman is sometimes called the goddess of black magic, but she is also known as the Celtic version of a witch. She had three sons who accompanied her named Dub, Dother, and Dain, whose names meant darkness, evil, and violence. She was a feared force because of her ability to ruin the well-being of the Irish people. She was eventually defeated by the members of the Tuatha De Danann, but before her defeat, she was said to come through Ireland and destroy the nation's crops. She and her sons would ravage all fruit, vegetables, and grains. In the lore, she was considered to be an invader from Greece. She was an all-consuming destructive force, and her defeat was a major joy for the Irish people because they didn't have to worry so much about the possible destruction of their crops. After all, kinder gods were protecting them from forces such as Carman.

Cat sìth

This creature is a catlike creature that originated in the Scottish Highlands. There are some versions of this in Ireland, but this is mostly a Scottish myth. It is commonly portrayed to be a black cat, with some white patches on its back. In some lore, this cat was a witch who was allowed to become a cat nine times, which is why even today people say that cats have nine lives. The Cat sìth is a large cat that haunts people. Some mythology claims that these cats were soul stealers because they would snatch the souls of the dead before the gods were able to do so. Some studies suggest that this cat was based on a real cat, the Kellas Cat, which is a wildcat native to Scotland, and it looks very much like the mythical cat. In any case, this mythological cat is not one you'd like to see in the wild because of its evil.

Cù sìth

Cù sìth is similar to the cat sìth, but it is a dog. As a ghost dog that is integral in Scottish myth, the Cù sìth is a formidable force. In Irish myths, this creature is generally called the Cu sidhe or the English call this creature the Hounds of Annwn. The Scottish name translates into 'fairy dog'. Interestingly, this creature was frequently associated with green-colored fur, which connected it to the fairy world. In Irish tradition, the dog was purely black. In some traditions, these creatures had flaming eyes. With paws the size of a man's hands, seeing this dog would have been a terrifying sight, and it made it even more frightening that this dog was associated with death because it would show up when people were about to die, similar to the Grim Reaper. Hearing it howling would be a horrific sign for Celtic people because that's how they knew that terrible occurrences were coming.

Dearg Due

Dearg Due is another version of a Celtic vampire, which also motivated Bram Stoker when he was making his book *Dracula*.

This monster arose in the middle portion of Ireland. The words Dearg Due mean 'red blood-sucker' in Irish. While Abhartach is a male vampire, Dearg Due is a female. This seductive woman would attract men and then steal their blood from then. Legend has it that the Dearg Due was once a woman who was in love with a poor, peasant man, but her father didn't think the man she loved was suitable. Accordingly, she was forced to marry a well-off man who was abusive and disrespectful to her. As a result, she was so unhappy and miserable that she later killed herself. Then, after she was buried, she rose from the dead, and her first victims were her husband and her father. She sucked all their blood out of them so that they would die. She was said to then rise again annually and attack other men. She was a terrifying creature to many Irish people, and she lives on through modern-day vampire stories.

Dullahan

The Dullahan is a monster whose name can be translated into "dark man" because of his haunting lore. He is a Celtic monster who, even today, is used in pop culture, particularly video games. He is the Irish's variation of the headless horseman, and he rides a black horse without his head. He carries his head as he rides, and his horse has fiery eyes. He is a predictor of death because whenever he comes to a stop, death will fall upon people. Some legends are more gruesome than others. In some, Dullahan would toss bloody buckets onto people, or as he rode, he would shout the names of the people who were going to die. In any case, this ominous monster caused a lot of nightmares for those who heard tales of this devious creature. In some myths, the Dullahan works in cahoots with the Banshee.

Ellén Trechend

This creature is a monster that has three heads. It is generally an Irish myth, but it may have existed in similar variations in other Celtic cultures as well. It was killed by a poet called Amergin mac Eccit, who was also a warrior. Before it was killed, it lived in a cave and caused havoc in Ireland. Some people say that this creature could turn into a bird, but it is unknown what it looked like in Celtic times.

Elves

You've surely heard of elves before, and the ones we know today are a composite of Irish and Norse myths, whose cultures both included elves. Elves are sometimes simply considered fairies, but it is interesting to consider the Celtic role in the little elves that still remain in modern fairytales and stories. Their original form was more mischievous than the Christmas elves you see in modern culture.

Enbarr

Enbarr is a Celtic mythological horse. The word means Enbarr means imagination, and generally, this horse is known to be either white or gray. It is said that Enbar had the skills to run over land or sea without her feet touching the ground or the water. This horse was often connected to female owners, but the exact owner of her is unclear.

Fear Gorta

The Fear Gorta is a terrifying Irish spirt that took the form of an emaciated man, which would be haunting for people to see because of the implications of this starving creature. He would often foretell famine, showing the doom and gloom that may be coming to people.

Fetch

The Fetch is a ghost-like creature that looks exactly like a human. Seeing a Fetch was considered a symbol of someone's impending death. The Fetch that looked like a dying person would come to warn of the death. This Irish creature is often associated with the Doppelgangers discussed in German lore. It is also sometimes associated with the English creature, the Wraith.

Finnbhennach

This creature is a bull that was owned by the King of Connacht in Irish mythology. This creature represents fertility because of how fertile it is in the legend, and it is an intimidating creature that you would not want to have to face.

Fomorians

Fomorians are a type of creature that is said to have predated the Irish gods found in the Tuatha de Danann. The gods were forced to take on this supernatural race before they could take over. Sometimes, they are either raiders or giants. The gods were able to beat these forces and keep them away.

Fuath

The Fuath is a type of Scottish creature that is associated with the word 'hate'. It's a nasty water creature that lives in the depths of waters and tries to lure people in and hurt them.

Glaistig

This is a Scottish creature that is half woman and half goat. In some legends, the woman part of this creature is gorgeous while, in others, she is a hag. She also is sometimes kind, while other times, she is considered to be an evil creature. Mostly, she is mischievous more than anything else and does minimal harm to people.

Kelpie

Kelpie is one of the most important creatures from Celtic myth. This creature is a shapeshifting monster, but it most commonly takes the form of a horse. It wanders around acting like a helpless horse to trick vulnerable women and kids into trying to ride it, but the unique aspect of this creature is its connection to water. Even when it's on land, the Kelpie would have a mane that was dripping with water. When it would get a victim to ride it, the Kelpie would trot the victim to the sea and go into the water, causing the rider to drown. In some retellings of the myth, the Kelpie would turn itself into a good-looking man to lure women to the water, but in these instances, the Kelpie would always have hair that was kelp. While the Kelpie would look harmless, this malevolent creature likes to kill as many victims as it can.

Leanan Sidhe

Lenan Sidhe is a mythical Irish creature that is both a muse to the fairies and a demonic creature. She is also similar to the other Celtic versions of vampires. Like many other creatures, she would take on a beautiful form and lure people back to her lair. To do this, she would provide them artistic inspiration in their art, music, or poetry. As she left the men that she beguiled, they would fall into a depression, and then they would die. Once the men were dead, she could take them back to her home base. She would drain them of their blood and put it into her huge, scarlet cauldron. The cauldron filled with the blood is what gave her her power, and she could use this power to then go and inspire more men's artistic pursuits before killing those men as well. She'd do this in an unending cycle of inspiring, killing, draining of blood, and starting all over again.

Merrow

A Merrow is the Irish version of mermaids and mermen. Interestingly, these creatures had green hair. They are connected to the sirens in other mythology. These creatures are prominent because they were used in Homer's *Odyssey*, which is an important piece of literature that included Celtic folklore. Sometimes, these creatures may be considered fairies. The males were generally thought to be ugly in comparison to the beautiful female Merrows. They'd both lure humans in and could become violent. Some legends say that they would remove the limbs of their victims.

Oilliphéist

The Cù sìth was a type of Oilliphést, but there are others. It is generally a water monster, but it is sometimes from Earth as well. Usually, it is a beast that has serpent-like qualities and often uses water to hurt people. These monsters are generally evil. They are similar to the well-known creature originating in the Scottish Highlands, the Lochness Monster, a water creature that people still claim to spot even today! This creature is also similar to the Questing Beast.

Questing Beast

The Questing Beast is a snake-like creature that would have different parts of animals as different body parts. He would often have the back of a lion, deer hooves, a snakehead, and a leopard's body. This creature was speedy, and it was loud. Legend says that the Questing Beast sounds like thirty barking dogs. Its bark was just as bad as its bite, and it terrorized people. In Arthurian legends, the lore would grow, and the beast would be hunted down by various knights. Thus, this legend is an important part of Celtic history and remains known widely by Celts even today.

Sluagh

Another Irish monster, the Sluagh, were the spirits of Irish sinners who had died. Their spirits group together, flying like birds to try to capture the souls of people who are dying. Because these vengeful spirits were said to come from the west, Irish people would often keep windows that were on the west side of their houses sealed to prevent the Sluagh from taking their souls. There are versions of this creature in some Scottish myths. Their name means horde, representing how they swarm in a large group before descending onto unsuspecting people.

These destructive beings have since been seen in video games and books, as well as on supernatural TV shows.

Unicorn

I'm sure that you know of Unicorns because they are one of the most enduring of Celtic creatures. Unicorns are horses that have horns and can sometimes fly. The Unicorn is so important to Scottish tradition that it is Scotland's national animal, even now despite being mythical. This creature has long been used to symbolize uniqueness and strength. Interestingly, it has also historically been used to symbolize masculinity, which is funny given that it is more associated with little girls in modern times. It also signifies purity, and in Christian times, was associated with the Virgin Mary. Some myths say that the unicorn would throw itself over the side of the cliff when it was being chased and would then land on its horn, which would top it from being wounded. Other legends reflect the purity associated with Unicorns. One myth discusses how noble maidens could capture Unicorns with their beauty. The Unicorn would be drawn in and would sleep with its head in the lap of the maiden, and accordingly, it would become the maiden's Unicorn despite loving its freedom. In Scotland, specifically, attributes such as free-spiritedness, intelligence, and courage are seen as some of the most admiral qualities of this creature. The Unicorn has even been used on currency and the Scottish coat of arms to symbolize the Scottish spirit. On the royal flag, the Unicorn is balanced against the lion, which is an English symbol.

Werewolves of Ossory

The Werewolves of Ossory are another Irish mythological group that has been linked with St. Patrick in Christian times. The tale stems from earlier tales of Werewolves, but this specific group of Werewolves was one that St. Patrick had to deal with as he was trying to convert to Celts to Christianity. It's said that upon stumbling onto a Celtic tribe who he wanted to convert, St. Patrick discovered that the men weren't like other men. They would howl at him as if they Werewolves, so because he was frustrated, St. Patrick prayed to God and asked him to punish these men for their reprehensible behavior. God then cursed the tribe and made them, and their ancestors, have to be Werewolves. They'd have to endure seven-year stretches as wolves. Some of the men were forced to become Werewolves every seven years rather than for seven years consecutively. While a Christian story, the Werewolves of Ossory shows that the types of mythology created by the Celts continued and adapted long into Christian times.

Chapter 5: Celtic Stories

The Oral Tradition

As you know, the Celtic tradition was carried on primarily through oral means until people finally began writing the stories down hundreds of years later. Thus, the original ways that these stories were told can only be speculated, but many are rooted in the wonderful imaginations of the Celtic tribes who created theological mythology. The druids passed down vital information and were keepers of these stories, and they did good work. Still, of course, nothing compares to the preservation skills of writing information down, but because Celtic writing was not advanced, they had to rely on verbally sharing information. Some stories have been observed by Romans, who did write the information down. However, the information we've ascertained from Romans may be skewed because the Romans did look down upon the Celts. Thus, some of what we know is shadowed by bias. Nevertheless, biased information from Julius Caesar and his company is better than nothing, and archeological finds help us piece together an even clearer picture. Further, some Christian stories often also tell us much about the Celtic ones that they were influenced by.

Sadly, many Celtic stories weren't written down until the 19th century. The following stories are either about Celtic mythological deities or are inspired by them and the Celtic religion that predated Christianity. These stories have creatures and figures that we've already discussed and were used to teach lessons about morality and the correct way to conduct oneself. Further, they were also used to explain the heroics and struggles of the Celtic people in the past, as well as to provide entertainment.

Popular Stories in Celtic Countries

Aengus' Plight

Aengus was the god of love. He is similar to the Greek's cupid. Though, he looks more rugged. He wasn't the most handsome of the gods, but he was a romantic.

The son of the Dagda and Boann, Aengus was the Irish god of youthfulness. While she was pregnant with Aengus, Boann cast a spell so that the sun wouldn't rise or set during the nine-month duration of her pregnancy. She did this because she was already married to Nechtan, and she didn't want him to know about her relationship with the Dagda. As a result, it seemed like Aengus was born on the same day that he was conceived.

In his myth, Aengus had a dream about the most beautiful woman that he had ever seen, named Caer. He fell in love with the woman in his dream, so much so that he became sick. He was unable to eat, so he became thin and weak. No matter what he did, he couldn't get the woman off his mind.

Eventually, he was able to find the woman he loved by the lake, but he realized that she was a swan. She was forced to be a swan after being cursed. She and the other girls would turn into swans every other year during Samhain.

Yet, despite hundreds of other swans being around, he recognized her right away. Because he was so in love, he decided that he would be a swan too, at least temporarily, to take her away. He had asked her father to marry her, but he had denied his request, so Aengus knew that he would have to sneak away with his love. He changed himself into a swan, and together they flew away and lived in Aengus' castle for the rest of their years.

Arthurian Legends

The Arthurian legends are some of the most prevalent legends of all time. They are set during the fourth and fifth centuries and have been reimagined and reinvented many times over. These legends are known for characters like King Arthur, Merlin, Lancelot, Morgan Le Fay, and Gawain, among many others. Most of these characters have roots dating back to Celtic times. Morgan, for example, has been linked to the Celtic Lady of the Lake. Further, other mythical elements find their way into these stories. In one story of Gwain that includes beheading, the beheading method mirrors Celtic rituals of beheading.

Further, in much of Arthurian legend, the Quest for the Holy Grail is important, and this holy grail is often associated with Christian beliefs, but it has also been linked to the Celtic term 'graal', which related to a story of the Fisher King, who is a disfigured monarch. This king is often associated with a character named Bran, who had a cauldron that helped him bring the dead back to life, which then became the Fisher King story. Thus, the Arthurian cauldron may be linked to this magical cauldron, rather than Jesus's cup as is sometimes posited.

Scholars have linked many other Celtic figures to Arthurian ones, so many of the gods and goddess align with the knights and royalty found in Arthurian legend. The origins of the Arthurian legends are murky, but there is no doubt that Celtic myths played some role in these famous tales.

Beast of Bodmin

According to Cornish legend, there's a beast that lives at Bodmin Moor. The beast is said the be a big, black cat that sort of resembles a panther, but it has extra scary yellow eyes that would surely intimidate anyone who saw it. This legend is an old one, but even today, the legend continues. In 1995, the Cornish government even investigated this creature's existence. They did not find any proof that it existed, but people still fear this wild cat.

Blodeuwedd

Blodeuwedd was a Welsh creature who was made out of flowers. She was created by the magicians Gwydion, and Math, on behalf of Lleu Llaw Gyffes. Lleu was an illegitimate child and was cursed by his mother when he was born so that he wouldn't have a wife, weapons, or even a name unless they were given to him by her. Because his mother was easily tricked, Lleu received a name and weapons when his uncle tricked his mother into granting them to him, but it was not as simple to get him a wife.

However, because Blodeuwedd wasn't human, she could be his wife!
Unfortunately for Lleu, Blodeuwedd did not have the same ethics as humans, and she cheated on Lleu. Blodeuwedd and her new man began to plot how they could kill Lleu. The

problem was that Lleu was protected and could only be killed in a certain way.

There was a riddle that said that he couldn't be killed during the day or night, nor indoors or outdoors, neither riding nor walking, not clothed and not naked, and not by any weapon lawfully made.

Unsure of how she would be able to kill him, Blodeuwedd tricked Lleu into revealing how he could be killed.
He revealed that he could only be killed during dusk, wrapped in a net, with one foot on a cauldron and one on a goat. On top of that, he had to be killed using a spear that had been forged for a whole year during the hours that everyone was at mass.

Blodeuwedd planned the murder meticulously, but it was unsuccessful. As Lleu was struck by the spear, he turned into an eagle and flew away. He was turned back into a human by Gwydion, who along with Math, nursed him back to health. As a punishment, Gwydion turned Blodeuwedd into an owl.

Bugganes

A buggane is a furry creature with black hair, sharp tusks, and fiery eyes. One of the main stories for this creature is the Buggane of St. Trinian's church. In this story, a buggane ended up on a boat that was headed to Ireland, but he wanted to go back to the Isle of Man. Accordingly, he created a storm that would send the ship back to the Isle of Man and that would possibly kill the sailors. It's said that St. Trinian redirected the ship and led the sailors to safety. The captain of the ship proclaimed that he would build a church in St. Trinian's honor. The buggane was angry, so each time a roof was put on the church, he would take it off. This happened three times.

Another famous buggane story is that of Finn MacCool. Finn was a giant who came into conflict with a buggane. He was not much of a fighter, and he had no interest in fighting, so instead, his wife made Finn look like a baby. This fooled the buggane into thinking that Finn's father was an extra-large giant because of how big his baby was. The buggane ran away, terrified of encountering a giant among giants. Eventually, they did end up fighting, and in the battle, Finn ripped out a tooth from his mouth to protect himself. He threw the tooth at the buggane, hitting him in the back of the head. The tooth bounced off his head, and landed in the sea, becoming a rock formation at the Isle of Man which is now known as Chicken Rock.

Children of Lir

The children of Lir is one of the most important Celtic stories of all. This story combines Christian messages with the mythology perpetuated by the druids in pre-Christian times. Some scholars suggest that this story was eventually the basis for the famous ballet *Swan Lake* (as is Aengus' story). This myth is beloved still, and it shows the merging of early Celtic culture with Christianity. This myth also represents a classic evil stepmother story that is a theme in many fairytales.

In the story, there was a king who ruled the sea. He was named Lir. With his wife, Eva, he had four children. A son, a daughter, and then two more sons. Eva died when her children were still young, so Lir thought that it would be good to find a new wife so that his children could have a mother. As a result, he wed Eva's sister, who was a magical being called Aoife. While Aoife was a good mother for a while, she quickly became jealous of the attention that Lir, a devoted father, gave to his four children. In her jealousy, Aoife took the children to a lake, and she cast a spell on them so that they would become swans. She hadn't wanted to kill them because she feared that killing them would lead to them haunting her. Thus, the children were made to live as swans for nearly a millennium. The curse specified that they would not be able to turn back into people until a bell rang, and St. Patrick came to Ireland.

Even under the spell, the children were still able to use their voices, so they would sing songs, and they could tell their father what Aoife had done to them. For obvious reasons, Lir was enraged and cast Aoife out of his country. Being so dedicated, Lir would return to the lake every day. After three hundred years, they moved onto a new lake and said goodbye to Lir.

Then, they traveled to a final lake after another three hundred years. Over this time, Lir had died, and his castle had become ruins, but the children finally heard the bell, which were the first Catholic bells. The swans found a home with a man named Caomhog who cared for them, but their peace was unsettled. The King of Connacht came to see the swans and tried to take them. Fortunately, the spell completed at that time, and the swans turned back into children. Terrified, the King of Connacht ran away. The kids were Christened into the Christian faith, but their bodies aged quickly, and they died shortly after.

Cornish Giants

In Cornish legend, they say that St. Michael's Mount was built by Cornish giants, particularly the giant Cormoran and his wife, Cormelian. These giants lived in the forest, and when they found granite, Cormelian is said to have carried the granite in her apron. Her husband made her lug the granite around, but it was heavy, so while her husband slept, she swapped it for greenstone. Before she completed the swap, he noticed what she was doing, and he kicked her. As a result, the strap on her apron broke, and the greenstone fell right where St. Michael's mount is. One night, while still on the mountain, Cormoran was slaughtered by Jack the Giant Killer, who took his head off with an ax. Thus, the boulders that are nearby are said to be; as a result, of this battle and other battles that Cormoran had.

Cu Chulainn's Birth

As one of the most infamous figures in Irish folklore, Cu Chulainn has a story of his own, but his birth also has a unique story that is famous in Celtic literature. Dechtire was the sister of King Conchobar, and she and her friends would take the form of a flock of birds. They would fly, and the group of maidens would vex the men. Hunters would attack them, but they would always escape. One day Dechtire met Lug, who was a god. Lug promised Dechtire that he wouldn't tell her brother that she was among the bird maidens who so irritated the men of Ulster. Lug told the king that his sister had been in the company of fair and lovely maidens instead. She then went on to give birth to Cu Chulainn, who Lug had put in her womb. There are several variations on this birth story, but this is one of the most prominent.

Cu Chulainn's Legend

The story of Cu Chulainn is another one of the most well-known Celtic myths because of the tragic heroism of the main character. Cu Chulainn was the nephew of the King of Ulster, and he was the son of Deichtne and Lugh, who was a god. Originally named Setanta, he acquired his new name after killing the guard dog of Culann. He killed the dog in self-defense and served as a protector for Culann until a replacement dog could be found, which is a major part of his story.

As a child, he often got himself into trouble due to being unaware of certain cultural norms. He'd meet new people, but would easily find trouble. In one such case, he didn't realize that he was supposed to ask for protection while playing in a field. As a result, he got attacked by other boys who thought that he was a threat. He ended up beating all the other boys, and King Conchobar stepped in and ended the fight, but he was impressed by Cu Chulainn, who had the skill to become a monster when under attack, which made him a powerful adversary for anyone who faced him.

As the story continued, King Conchobar was invited to dinner with Culann, and being so in awe of Cu Chulainn, the king took Cu Chulainn with him to the dinner. When they arrived at Culann's house, Culann's guard dog attacked, which resulted in Cu Chulainn killing the dog. While he could have a monstrous side, Cu Chulainn felt responsible for his actions and strived to make his mistake right by guarding Culann in the interim.

One day when he was at school being taught by the druids, one druid, Cathbad, said that any pupil who took on a weapon during that day would have notoriety. Because he wanted that fame, Cu Chulainn decided that he would go to King Conchobar to ask for weapons. All the weapons he tried, he broke because he was too strong, and this was when he was only seven years old, which makes it even more remarkable. Eventually, the king gave Cu Chulainn his own weapon, but Cu Chulainn hadn't listened to the entire prophecy. What he didn't hear was that the person who took on a weapon would be destined to have a short life despite the fame.

When he became older, Cu Chulainn wanted to marry the daughter of a man named Forgall, but Forgall actually had plans to kill Cu Chulainn. Cu Chulainn found other marriage prospects, and one was Scarthach, who was a female warrior who taught Cu Chulainn how to fight. Cu Chulainn came face to face with another warrior woman, and he impregnated her. Despite all of this, he still pined for Forgall's daughter, Emer. He returned to Scotland to see his beloved Emer, but her father still wasn't allowing him to marry his daughter. Angry that he couldn't have the woman he wanted, Cu Chulainn attacked Forgall's castle. Forgall ended up falling and dying. Cu Chulainn also killed many others, and he kidnapped Emer. With treasure looted from Forgall, he began a life with Emer, but there was one small problem. King Conchobar, as the king had the right to have the first night sleeping with women in any marriage in his kingdom. He didn't want to enrage Cu Chulainn, but if he didn't sleep with Emer, he'd lose respect among his citizens. Thus, the king made a deal with the druid Cathbad that he could sleep in the bed with Emer, but Cathbad would sleep in the middle of them so as to not enrage Cu Chulainn.

Eventually, a group of men conspired to kill Cu Chulainn. They were all the offspring of men that Cu Chulainn had killed. These men did eventually kill him, but before he died, he tied himself to a stone, so that he could be standing and facing his enemies as he died. Fulfilling the prophecy that the druid had foretold, he had become infamous, but he was still young when he died.

Fionn Mac Cumhaill

Fionn Mac Cumhaill is one of the most prominent Celtic warriors. He led a group of fighters called the Fianna, and these warriors were so outstanding that the Irish named one of their political parties, the Fianna Fail, after these warriors. In his early years, Fionn spent time with a poet named Finnegas, who wanted to find the Salmon of Knowledge, a fish that contained all Earth's knowledge because he had eaten hazelnuts that had fallen in a well of wisdom.

Finnegas found the fish, and he gave it to Fionn, telling him not to eat it. Despite what Finnegas had instructed, Fionn decided that he would fry the fish. However, when he went to cook it, he accidentally burned his finger. He put his finger in his mouth to reduce the burn, and the taste of fish that he got was enough that he was suddenly filled with knowledge. When Finnegas found out what happened, he allowed Fionn to eat the whole fish. Whenever Fionn bit his tongue, he could call upon his knowledge and know anything that he wanted, which is one of the most impressive feats in the entire collection of Celtic mythology.

There's one other story of Fionn that is incredibly important in Celtic myths. On another occasion, when he was a little older, he had to hunt down a demon that breathed fire and burnt down a castle on Samhain. The demon would make the soldiers fall asleep, and then defeat them as they slept, but Fionn outsmarted the demon by putting a hot piece of metal to his forehead so that he would stay awake. His victory over the demon made him famous as one of the most courageous and most intelligent heroes of all Celtic mythology.

Legend of Lough Gur

A man named Larry Cotter was a farmer with land in Lough Gur. He was living a good life, at least for the most part. He lived a normal life, doing nothing too adventurous, and preferred the quiet of home. Unfortunately for him, things slowly took a turn for the worse. Each year, his agricultural endeavors would be ruined when his grass was destroyed. He asked his neighbor named Tom what he should do about the situation. Tom answered that the situation was bad all around and that he should try to watch at night to see if any cattle came onto his grass.

Thus, Larry, with the help of his two sons, stayed out and watched for any issues. Then, he heard something from the water, and he told his sons to be quiet and stay put. As they patiently waited, they saw a huge cow emerge near the lake. The cow had 7 white heifers with it. Along with his sons, he was able to capture the 7 heifers and took them to the pound. After three days, no owner had come forth and so Larry took them for himself. He put the heifers in a field of his own, and for a short time his problem was solved.

However, one morning he went out to his field and all 7 heifers were gone without a trace. The gate was left open, and it appeared as though they had returned to the lake from where they came. Thus, Larry got no relief and was in for more misery. The cows continued to ruin his crops, and he was never able to grow anything on his land. He became a drunkard, and later died from alcoholism.

Rhiannon

Rhiannon is a character who appears in the Mabinogion in the First Branch. In Wales, there was said to be a *gorsedd*, which is a magical mound that will provide either something awful or something wonderful to whoever sat upon it. A lord, Pwyll, sat on this mound one day, and saw a breathtaking woman on a horse. She was wearing white, and her horse was white too, making her look even more beguiling. He had his men try to stop her, but she was faster than any of his men, so he decided that he had to chase her himself.

He yelled at her desperately, hoping that she would see him. When she heard him, she stopped her horse so that they could talk. She introduced herself as Rhiannon. She and Pwyll fell in love, but they feared that they were under a curse because they were unable to have children. While they did eventually have a son, more misery would befall them. The day before the festival of Beltane, their son was kidnapped. The people on watch had fallen asleep, and because they did not want to get in trouble, they killed a puppy and put the blood on Rhiannon so that it would look as though she had killed her child and eaten him as well. Pwyll punished Rhiannon by having her stay by the gate of their estate, and every time someone came to visit, she had to carry them up the steps on her back. Fortunately, their child was later found, and he was taken back to Pwyll and Rhiannon.

The child was named Pryderi. While in this tale, Rhiannon was just a woman on a horse, she was referred to as the goddess of horses back in pagan times. Her story could have ended tragically as so many do, but for once, a tragic start has a good ending.

The Craig-y-don Blacksmith

The Craig-y-don Blacksmith is a Welsh legend in which fairies are used as benevolent creatures who convince people to do what is moral. In this story, a blacksmith lived in Craig-y-don. Unfortunately, the blacksmith was a heavy drinker, and he'd get far too drunk.

One day, when he was drunk by a river, tiny men appeared from the rocks. The oldest one spoke to the blacksmith and told him that if he kept on the same course that he would die from his vices, but if he decided to change his life, that good things would end up happening to him. Upon telling the blacksmith this prophecy, the fairies disappeared back into the rocks.

When the fairy men disappeared, the blacksmith decided that he would listen to their advice, and he started to change his life. He stopped drinking himself to death, and he no longer spent his nights getting drunk. Shortly after he changed his ways, the blacksmith was nailing a horseshoe to a man's horse. The horse bolted, and in doing so pulled down part of the wall of his shop. He never saw the horse again, but while fixing the masonry he found 3 kettles full of gold. This story was used to teach people that they would be rewarded for prudent behaviors. It is one of several Welsh tales that uses fairies as purveyors of morals.

The Fairies of Caragonan

As the story goes, fairies once lived in a place called Mona. In Mona, the Queen of the Fairies' daughter was fifteen years old when she told her mother that she wanted to learn more about the world and explore it a bit more. She wanted to see the outside world because she felt too sheltered. Her mother agreed that she could leave for one day, and she was permitted to switch between being a bird and a fairy as she pleased.

The daughter came back to Mona, and she was very upset when she told her mother that she found a man who was very ill. The daughter's mother looked into the young man, and the queen realized that the man had been cursed. The queen agreed to cure the young man of the curse. She and her band of fairies cast a spell. They took a blue pot, and they put perfume in it. Then, they set the pot on fire. With her spell, she was able to cure the man, and in exchange she asked for him to build three walls facing the sea on his land. This was to be a place that the fairies could come and go as they pleased. Gratefully, the cured man obliged, and built the three walls.

The story did not end there, though. In the second part, the way the man got cursed is detailed. The man happened to live near a witch. The witch could turn into a hare whenever she wanted to. The man was excellent at hunting these hares, but he could never get the ugly, old witch. He hit her with a whip one day, and she cursed him, and he became incredibly sick. After that, he was cured by the fairies.

In the third part, the queen went back home to talk to her daughter about what had happened, and she told her daughter that she wouldn't have power to kill the old witch for a year. In order for the witch to be defeated for good, a man would have to do the killing. With this knowledge in mind, the fairy daughter left her home to see if she could find someone who would be able to kill the witch. During her search, the fairy daughter came across a man whose cows had been made sick by the witch. The fairy's daughter reported back to her mother, who cured the man's cows with her band of fairies and a spell. For her kindness, the fairy told the man that in exchange, she wanted him to come to the plot of land that she had gotten from the first man she cured.

In the fourth part of this tale, the queen and her daughter brought three hundred fairies together on the plot of land they were gifted. They used tape, a mirror, and a pole to prepare their trap for the dreaded witch. The witch told the man she saved to look at the mirror and say what he saw. He looked in the mirror, and in it he saw a hare running towards the mill. The queen then announced that there would be a hunt for the hare – the witch.

In the next section of the story, the fairy gives the man a slingshot to hunt with. She blessed the man and his weapon, and then instructed him to hunt the witch. The next day, he slung his pebble, and it hit the witch in the head, killing her once and for all.

The fairy instructed the brave man to meet her again the following day, at their 3-walled building by the beach. Once again, she was joined by 300 fairies, and together they instructed the man to look in their mirror.

This time, he saw a cupboard in the mirror. The fairy queen told him that he would see this cupboard for sale in town, and that he should buy it.

He did as the fairy queen instructed, and inside the cupboard he found a secret compartment, full of gold.

This was his reward for his bravery!

This story teaches that those who do good deeds and stand up to evil will be rewarded for their actions. It was meant to show that morality leads to good fortune. That fortune may come after hardship, but it comes to those who deserve it.

The Harp of the Dagda

After a battle at Moy Tura, the king of the Tuatha De Danann, King Nuada, was hurt, and because the rules stated that the king had to be able to use his entire body, the Dagda became the acting king. Of the wonderful artifacts that he had, one of these objects was a harp that was called Uaithne and played Four-Angled music. The harp was the most impressive of the Dagda's objects because with it not only could he prepare the warriors for battle, but he also could control the seasons. His harp was a thing of beauty that had been made from oak and was encrusted with jewels. The tone of the music could influence people's moods and the natural world.

The Dagda was fighting the Fomorians, and when they heard the beauty of its music, they desperately wanted to make the harp their own. Thus, they waited until the Dagda was unsuspecting and snuck into his house to steal the harp. While they were stealing the harp, they had left their own king, King Balor, alone on the battlefield. As a result, Balor was killed, but the Fomorians still had their harp to provide some comfort.

After the battle in which Balor was killed, the Dagda discovered that the harp had disappeared. The Dagda lamented the harp's vanishing, but he mentioned that it would not play nice music for the person who took it because only he could make it play beautiful songs. Ogma and Lugh joined the Dagda to retrieve the harp. When they got to where the Fomorians were, the Dagda called out to the harp and hearing his voice, the harp removed itself from the wall, hitting the Fomorians and returning to its owner. It slew seven of the Fomorians in addition to several other casualties.

The Dagda then used the harp to play some music that made the Fomorians start to laugh. They were so amused that the weapons they were holding clattered to the floor. The music stopped, and the Fomorians grabbed their weapons again, but then the Dagda started to play melancholy music, making the Fomorians cry because of grief for their lost soldiers. They went to attack, but as they moved forward, the Dagda played one last song. He played them a lullaby, and while they tried not to sleep, they could not resist the sweet harp's tune. After that day of victory, no entity ever tried to take the Dagda's harp.

The Moddey Dhoo

The Moddey Dhoo is a legend that originated in the Isle of Man. It is a story about a creature who was a big black dog. It is said that this hound haunts Peel Castle. It is said that the dog would run throughout the castle and appear in every room, only coming out at night. In one story, a guard had a terrifying encounter with this creature. He went around and locked the castle by himself. He heard noises, and then, he was left feeling shaky and pale when he got back to the guard room. The guard didn't mention what he saw, but everyone could tell that something was incredibly wrong. Three days after the encounter, the man died. As a result, they sealed up the passages that the hound was known to frequent, and the creature was never seen again as the legend goes.

Tir na Nog

Tir na Nog is the name of the Irish Otherworld. It is seen in the Tuatha De Danann. It's a wonderful paradise that is like the Christian idea of heaven. It is filled with art, music, and poetry. In myths, the heroes from the Tuatha De Dannan like to visit this place. They'd enter it commonly through either caves or mounds. They'd have to go through water, go across the sea, and walk through a mist to get there. In some stories, humans would take trips to Tir na Nog, and in these tales, it can be risky for mortals to go there despite the Otherworld being a paradise.

In one legend, a human, Oisin, and a woman who lives in the Otherworld, Niamh, loved each other. Oisin lived in the Otherworld before, but he wanted to go back to Ireland after three years in the Otherworld. His lover sent him back on a horse, but she warned that his feet could never touch the ground. He was in Ireland for three hundred years before he fell off the horse. Because he touched the ground, he started to grow old speedily, and, as a result, he died. There are similar stories to this in several other Celtic counties that express the same fundamental story, but this legend is the most well-known one.

Various other stories occur in Tir na nOg, and it has been seen in forms of pop culture such as literature, comic strips, music, film, video games, and television.

Tristram and Iseult

This story is one of the most well-known Cornish tragic legends. Tristram was the nephew of the Cornish King, King Mark. He was hurt in a battle in which he killed the Irish queen's brother. No one expected that he would live, so they put him on a boat and didn't give him any sails. Luckily for him, the boat did reach the shores, and he was found and nurtured by Iseult, who was the daughter of the Irish king. The young man and woman fell in love. Unfortunately, despite being in love, fate was not kind to the lovers because they could not be wed. After all, Tristram had killed the queen's brother. He was sent away from Ireland, and he and Iseult each had to marry other people, but they remained in love. Ironically, Tristram's wife was also named Iseult, but he never loved her like he loved his first Iseult. Thinking that his Iseult had died due to lies told by Tristram's envious wife, Tristram ended up dying of a broken heart. This story is fundamentally a Cornish version of Romeo and Juliet. While tragic, this story shows the beautiful dedication of true love.

Chapter 6: The Lingering Influence of Celtic Myths

The Fall of the Celtic Religion

In the years 400 to 250 BCE, the Celts reached their peak of power, and their influences could be seen across Europe, but as the Romans became more powerful, the Celts began to have less influence, particularly in Europe. They also lost the battle to Christianity. Not only did Julius Caesar drive the Celts away, but tribes from Germany also attacked the Celt people, causing their influence to decline further. Despite the decrease in Celtic prominence, many of the impacts of Celtic culture existed long after the decline of the religion. In the years 500 to 1000 CE, Christianity and Celtic influences began to merge. People who live in Celtic areas are still called Celtic today, even though their myths have evolved and shifted over the years, as have their culture.

The fall of the Celtic religion was unfortunate because many myths and stories were lost in the transition. These stories weren't carried over because the Celts did not write down their mythology. Many of the retellings of mythical stories are done through a Christian lens, which didn't capture the full nuance of the stories and traditions. Some of the languages died, and many of the stories will continue to die out unless they are continued to be talked about and written down.

Cultural Impacts of Celts

The Celtic languages often define the Celtic culture, but some things exist today that we refer to as Celtic that have been created based purely on Celtic principles. In some areas, Celtic prominence has waxed and waned, but presently, many countries are trying to revive and relearn Celtic traditions that tie them back to their roots. Some governments have made efforts to relearn the languages, and festivals and celebrations have been established to learn and expand upon Celtic culture in Celtic countries.

One of the most interesting influences of Celtic culture is the influence of the druids. As you know, the druids were fundamentally the Celtic version of priests, but they had even more responsibilities and were more esteemed. They were the intellectual group of Celts, and they did not have to fight in wars, so their primary role was to further the wisdom of their tribes. The Celts loved learning and knowledge despite also being incredibly superstitious and full-heartedly believing in their myths. While they had a rudimentary written language, the druidic system mostly encouraged learning through oral tradition. The information would be repeated and passed down orally, meaning that there were no written sources of the Celtic culture other than that of the Romans. Because the Celtic people had to rely on memorization, they needed mental acuity and academic focus, which the druids encouraged. They helped people be self-disciplined so that they could accomplish the required learning to maintain the culture. Thus, when the Celts began being converted to Christianity, they carried this work ethic and academic style along with them. As a result, Celtic art thrived under Christianity and had a renaissance during the period of conversion. This artwork was rooted in the tradition of passing down language and having an intellectual focus.

The Celtic people not only began serving in Christian roles and incorporating themselves into that religion, but they also held roles in royal courts. Due to their excellent academic history, despite not writing anything down, they were called upon by royals as advisors. They'd advise on religion, law, disputes, and foreign affairs because of their wisdom. They became important parts of the communities that they were integrated into because of their wonderful cultural contributions and knowledge. Groups like the Romans looked down on the Celts sometimes for being lesser, but in actuality, the Celts were one of the most interesting groups of their time.

One of the most notable influences of Celtic culture is the Celtic knot, which is a type of illustration style that looks like a knot. If you look this term up, you can find thousands of designs that show the intricacy and beauty of this art form. This art form was seen during the Roman empire, but even before Christian and Roman influences, early patterns of Celtic knot art could be found. Christians later used these patterns to illustrate books. This art continues to be an important part of Celtic culture today.

Celtic art was an important part of the culture for the Celtic tribes. They regularly created murals, sculptures, and mosaics. They were also known for being great blacksmiths and shaping metal weapons that they'd offer to the gods and use for other traditional religious practices. Because so little is known about the religious traditions of the Celts, what we know about these influences is also limited, but they are clearly seen if you look at the transition to Christianity. Iron and metal work done by the Celts added to important areas of European development, but today, we know that these pieces often have religious and artistic roots because making weapons was often seen as an art form. Today, those important weapons are displayed among artistic collections.

Celtic music is still heard today, and many musical groups carry on the Celtic music tradition in the counties that still encourage Celtic culture. The music sounds a little different in each of the six (seven if you include Galicia in Spain) cultures that still honor the early Celts. Even places like the United States and Canada have Celtic inspired music because of immigration, and in these regions, the Celtic traditions are less pure and have been watered down, but they still exist, nevertheless. Music created in Celtic counties is often still considered Celtic even if it is distant from that of Celtic tribes and has more modern influences. Some of the instruments that are commonly used in Celtic music are bagpipes, the fiddle, accordions, banjos, harps, dulcimers, guitars, mandolins, flutes, and pennywhistles.

A Celtic cross is something that Christians took as their own. It's a cross that commonly has a ring around it. Unfortunately, this symbol has been used for malevolent purposes. During World War II, Nazis used their own version of this cross, and other white supremacists also began using this cross as their symbol. In the United States, for example, this cross has been used by the bigots of the hateful Ku Klux Klan. Stormfront, a major white supremacist group, also uses this cross as its icon. While this symbol has been taken over by undeserving parties, for a long time, it was merely a religious symbol that was also a representation of Irish pride. Thus, despite uses by awful people, this cross is more commonly associated with Celtic people celebrating their heritage and is not a racist symbol outside of the context of religious racist organizations. The racist groups usually use a round version of this cross, while Celts usually use an elongated cross instead of the sun cross, which adds some further distinction between the groups.

Even sports teams have been linked to the Celts. The basketball team in the United States, the Boston Celtics, was named after the Celtic culture in 1946. This team was named after an original New York team that went by the same name. The name was decided upon when the owner of the team, Walter Brown and his colleague Howie Mchugh discussed what the team should be named. Being of Irish ancestry, Mchugh had just returned from a trip to Ireland. Thus, considering how many people in Boston also had Irish ancestry, he suggested the Celtics so they could reflect that culture. Brown quickly agreed because the name could connect to the initial New York Celtics team that had been prevalent in the 1920s. Many sports teams in Celtic countries also are named the Celtics.

The tradition of Halloween across the world stems from the ancient Celts, who celebrated the holiday of Samhain, which became what we now know as Halloween. Because the Celts would start their holidays the eve before the feast day, all Hallow's Eve correlates to the start of that holiday. The Celtic holidays were carried on even in Catholicism. November 1, the day after Halloween, is known to Catholics as All Saint's Day, which mourns the loss of the dead. The word Halloween wasn't used until the 1800s, but the Celtic roots are undeniable.

Celtic culture is something that began to dwindle with the integration of Christianity, but even now, Celtic languages, traditions, and beliefs influence Celtic and global populations. The words of the Celts are still spoken, and that's a beautiful thing to hear. Some tongues of Celtic languages have unfortunately gone extinct, but the spirit of Celts lives on through those who still speak the languages that do exist.

It would be a real shame if these legends and beautiful stories died, so I urge you to spread what you have learned and continue to appreciate this wonderful culture. There are so many stories that have not been included here because of how long and varied the Celtic history is. Celtic mythology is a topic that is not just for academics. It is something that everyone can appreciate and develop a passion for. While these stories are often old fashioned and packed full of morals of the time in which they were created, in many ways, they feel timeless, and many people today can relate to these Celtic stories.

The Celtic culture has had such an influence on people across the world. Many people don't even realize that their traditions, stories, and art often have Celtic roots. The next time you hear stories of fairies or leprechauns, think of the early Celtic people who established these tales to make sense of the world. When you see a Celtic knot style artwork, think of how historical that art is. Even if you are not Celtic, you can understand the wonders of this beautiful culture and continue to learn and appreciate its roots and myths. The myths have been passed down for hundreds of years, and they only grow more charming and intriguing as time goes on.

Conclusion

Thank you for making it through to the end of *Celtic Mythology*! I hope you found it to be informative and able to provide you with all of the tools you need to achieve your goals, whatever they may be.

Some of the least known mythology is Celtic. While Greek and Roman mythology both get a plethora of attention, less is known about Celtic myths. Nevertheless, Celtic myths are just as rich and entertaining as the myths of other cultures, and they have unique elements that deserve to be appreciated. Counties like Ireland, Scotland, England, and even France all have some Celtic roots, at least in parts of their countries. Thus, for many people, Celtic traditions still hold a great deal of meaning.

Beyond this book, there is an extensive amount of modern and historic Celtic culture that you can discover. While this book primarily focused on mythology because of how integral mythology was in all parts of Celtic life, there's even more to discover! I hope that this book has awakened you to the broad expanse of Celtic myths, and all that the Celtic culture has to offer you!

www.ingramcontent.com/pod-product-compliance
Lightning Source LLC
LaVergne TN
LVHW011722060526
838200LV00051B/2995